WOMEN
AND
THE PRIESTHOOD

WOMEN
AND
THE PRIESTHOOD

Edited by
THOMAS HOPKO

ST. VLADIMIR'S SEMINARY PRESS
CRESTWOOD, NEW YORK 10707
1983

Library of Congress Cataloging in Publication Data
Main entry under title:

Women and the priesthood.

Includes bibliographical references.
1. Ordination of women—Addresses, essays, lectures.
2. Ordination of women—Orthodox Eastern Church—Addresses,
essays, lectures. 3. Orthodox Eastern Church—Doctrinal and
controversial works—Addresses, essays, lectures. I. Hopko, Thomas.
BV676.W546 1983   262'.14   83-6657
ISBN 0-88141-005-5

© Copyright 1983

by

ST. VLADIMIR'S SEMINARY PRESS

The article "The Spirit of the Female Priesthood" by
Deborah Belonick is copyrighted © 1981 by
Deborah Belonick. Reprinted with permission.

ISBN 0-88141-005-5

PRINTED IN THE UNITED STATES OF AMERICA
BY
ATHENS PRINTING COMPANY
NEW YORK, NY

Contents

Preface

The authors of the articles and essays collected in this book do not pretend to have exhausted or even simply to have touched upon all the important questions raised by the decision of some Western Christian communions to admit women to the ordained ministry. It is rather a very preliminary, very tentative, reaction to a problem which, since the Orthodox Church has never faced it existentially, remains for her a *casus irrealis*. We are, however, asked "to be ready always to give an answer to every man that asks us a reason of the hope that is in us" (1 Pt 3:15). We cannot consider this extremely important matter as simply alien to us and, therefore, to be ignored—hence, this beginning of an answer, however tentative and fragmentary.

Three essential points, it seems to me, constitute the foundation of this answer. In the first place is the affirmation, common to all Orthodox theologians, of the impossibility of isolating the problem of women's ordination from the totality of the Church's *Tradition*, from the faith in the triune God, in the creation, fall and redemption, in the Church and the mystery of her "theandric" life. Once more the question of tradition stands at the very center and challenges us with essential questions. What is it? Is it the living memory and consciousness of the Church, the essential term of reference or criterion by which we discern the essential unbrokenness of the Church's life and identity during her pilgrimage through history? Or is it itself a product, or a sequence of products, of history, in the light of which it is to be reevaluated, judged, used or rejected?

In the second place, Orthodox theology is unanimous, I am sure, in affirming that the question of women's ordina-

tion must be seen and discussed within the scriptural doctrine of man and woman, i.e., of Christian scriptural and
doctrinal *anthropology*, and not within the perspective of
"human rights," "equality," etc.—categories whose ability
to adequately express the Christian understanding of man
and woman is, to say the least, questionable.

And this takes us to the third essential context: that of
ecclesiology, of the understanding of the Church and the
mystery of salvation. As presented today, it is the result
of too many reductions. For if its root is surrender to
culture, its pattern of development is shaped by *clericalism*.
Clericalism is, on the one hand, the reduction of the
Church to a power structure; and on the other hand, her
reduction of that power structure to *clergy*. Thus, the alleged
inferiority of women within secular society corresponds to
their inferiority within the ecclesiastical power structure,
their exclusion from the "clergy." And therefore, to their
liberation in secular society must correspond their liberation in the Church, i.e., their admission to the priesthood,
etc.

The Church simply cannot be reduced to these categories.
As long as we try to measure the ineffable mystery of her
life by concepts and ideas a priori alien to her very essence,
we *mutilate* her and her real power, glory and beauty. Her
real life simply escapes us.

It is my hope that the serious reader, whether agreeing
or disagreeing with the approach of the Orthodox Church
to the ordination of women, will try to understand this
approach as expressed in this book, however inadequately,
and will realize its true scope and significance.

Fr. Alexander Schmemann
Crestwood, N.Y.
January 1983

Man, Woman
and
the Priesthood of Christ

By Bishop
KALLISTOS WARE*

The Three Widows

If we had been visiting a church beside the Nile soon after the year 300, what kind of a parish ministry might we have found? For an answer, let us turn to the fragmentary document known as the *Apostolic Church Order*. This begins by mentioning the bishop, who is not yet a distant administrator, but still the immediate head of the local community, the normal celebrant at the Sunday eucharist. He is assisted in the parish worship by two or more presbyters, by a reader and by three deacons. Thus far there are no great surprises, except that the reader seems to rank higher than the deacons. The parochial staff is larger than what is customary today; but, apart perhaps from the bishop, most of the others are doubtless earning their own living with ordinary jobs. The *Apostolic Church Order* does not stop, however, with the deacons. After them it goes on to speak of three widows, "two to persevere in prayer for all who are in temptation,

*Kallistos Ware is Bishop of Diokleia for the Ecumenical Patriarchate of Constantinople in Great Britain. A professor at Oxford and a monk of the Monastery of St. John on Patmos, Bishop Kallistos is a leading spokesman for Orthodoxy in the West. His published works include the popular books *The Orthodox Church* and *The Orthodox Way*. The following article originally appeared in *Man, Woman, Priesthood*, ed. Peter Moore (London: Fletcher and Son, 1978) 68-90.

and to receive revelations when such are needed; and one to help the women who are ill."[1]

There are surely several things to interest us here. First of all we observe the size and diversity of the local parish ministry. There is no clericalism, no concentration of responsibility exclusively in the hands of a single, full-time "professional." Next, we see that the ministry includes women as well as men. The three widows are not just elderly ladies who arrange the flowers and prepare cups of tea, but they constitute a specific ministry or order recognized by the Church; they are more or less equivalent—although not actually given such a title—to the deaconesses mentioned elsewhere in early Christian sources. While one of the three is entrusted with charitable or social work, the other two have tasks immediately connected with prayer and worship. It is noteworthy that the particular role assigned to them is the ministry of intercession and prophecy. Although it is the calling of every Christian, male as well as female, to pray for others and to listen to God, yet woman by virtue of her gift for direct and intuitive understanding seems especially blessed to act as intercessor and prophet. It is no coincidence that the symbolic figure of the *Orans* on the walls of the Catacombs, representing the Christian soul waiting upon the Spirit, should take the form of a woman.

But the widows, although they intercede and receive revelations, do not act as celebrants at the eucharist. On this point the *Apostolic Church Order* is entirely clear: "When the Master prayed over the bread and the cup and blessed them, saying, 'This is my Body and Blood,' he did not allow women to stand with us."[2] Here the *Apostolic Church Order* agrees with the constant testimony of the universal Church, Eastern and Western, from apostolic times onward: women are entrusted with a wide variety of ministries, but they *do not perform the consecration at the eucharist*. To quote the standard code of eastern church law, the *Nomocanon* of

[1]A. Harnack, *Die Quellen der sogenannten apostolischen Kirchenordnung,* Texte und Untersuchungen, 2:5 (Leipzig 1886) 22-4; English translation by J. Owen, *Sources of the Apostolic Canons* (London 1895) 19-21.
[2]Harnack, 28 (Eng. tr., 25).

Photius: "A woman does not become a priestess."[3]

To an Orthodox Christian it seems not so much ironic as tragic that, at the very moment when Christians everywhere are praying for unity, we should see a new chasm opening up to divide us. And in Orthodox eyes, at any rate, it is a chasm of horrifying dimensions. "The ordination of women to priesthood," writes Fr. Alexander Schmemann, "is tantamount for us to a radical and irreparable mutilation of the entire faith, the rejection of the whole Scripture, and, needless to say, the end of all 'dialogues.'" He goes on to speak about "the threat of an irreversible and irreparable act which, if it becomes reality, will produce a new, and this time, I am convinced, final division among Christians."[4] According to another Orthodox spokesman, Fr. Thomas Hopko, the acceptance of women priests involves "a fundamental and radical rejection of the very substance of the biblical and Christian understanding of God and creation. . . . The decisions taken by the Episcopal Church in America at its General Convention in Minneapolis . . . can only be considered by an Orthodox Christian as disastrous."[5] These are strong words. Yet Frs. Schmemann and Hopko are both priests with long pastoral experience in the West, and both have the reputation within their own communion of being, in the best sense, progressive and open-minded. Why do they and other Orthodox feel so deeply?

In common with the recent Roman Catholic statement on "Women and the Priesthood" (*Inter Insigniores,* October 15, 1976), we Orthodox are influenced chiefly by two factors: the *witness of tradition* and the *"iconic" character of the Christian priesthood.* Beyond this we appeal also to the *"order of nature,"* to what the *Apostolic Constitutions,* when discussing the ministry of women, term the "ἀκολουθία τῆς φύσεως."[6]

[3]*Nomocanon* 1:37 (ed. G.A. Rallis and M. Politis, *Syntagma* 1:81). Priestess in Greek is πρεσβυτέρα.

[4]"Concerning Women's Ordination: Letter to an Episcopal Friend," in H. Karl Lutge, ed., *Sexuality-Theology-Priesthood* (San Gabriel, no date) 12-3.

[5]In the periodical of the Orthodox Church in America, *The Orthodox Church* (November 1976) 5.

[6]*Apostolic Constitutions* 3:9:4 (ed. Funk, 201).

But, when employing these three interdependent lines of argument, it is essential to make some careful distinctions: (1) Tradition is not to be equated with custom or social convention; there is an important difference between "traditions" and Holy Tradition. (2) The ministerial priesthood or priesthood of order is not to be confused with the royal priesthood exercised by all the baptized. (3) The order of nature does not signify fallen human nature, which is in reality profoundly *un*natural; it signifies true human nature as first created by God, the undistorted image as it existed before the fall.

The Appeal to Tradition

"We should hold fast," writes St. Vincent of Lérins, "to what has been believed everywhere, always and by everyone."[7] If ever there was a practice that contravened the Vincentian canon, it is certainly the ordination of women to the priesthood. Christ and the apostles and ministers of the early Church, as well as their episcopal and presbyteral successors throughout the ages, were men and not women. In a matter of such grave importance, do we have the right to act differently from them?

This appeal to tradition requires, however, careful handling. The New Testament, we are sometimes told, does not encourage Christians to think that nothing should be done for the first time. Loyalty to tradition must not become simply another form of fundamentalism. Tradition is dynamic, not static and inert. It is received and lived by each new generation in its own way, tested and enriched by the fresh experience that the Church is continually gaining. In the words of Vladimir Lossky, tradition is "the critical spirit of the Church."[8] It is not simply a protective, conservative principle, but primarily a principle of growth and regeneration. It is not merely a collection of documents, the record of what others

[7] *Commonitorium Primum* 2:3 (PL 50:640).
[8] *In the Image and Likeness of God* (Crestwood, N.Y.: SVS Press, 1974) 156.

have said before us, handed down automatically and repeated mechanically; but it involves a living response to God's voice at the present moment, a direct and personal meeting on our part, here and now, with Christ in the Spirit. Authentic traditionalism, then, is not a slavish imitation of the past, but a courageous effort to discriminate between the transitory and the essential. The true traditionalist is not the integrist or the reactionary, but the one who discerns the "signs of the times" (Mt 16:3)—who is prepared to discover the leaven of the gospel at work even within such a seemingly secular movement as "women's lib."

Yet, even when full allowance has been made for all this, it seems altogether insufficient to justify such a drastic innovation as women priests. If there is dynamism in Holy Tradition, there is also continuity. "Jesus Christ is the same yesterday, and today, and for ever" (Heb 13:8). The Spirit is always active in each new generation of the Church, yet it is the Spirit's role to bear witness to the Son (Jn 16:13-15); the Spirit brings us not a new revelation, but the eternal and unchanging truth of Christ himself. *Nove, non nova*, enjoins St. Vincent of Lérins:[9] we are not to do or to say "new things," for the revelation brought by Christ is final and complete. But, guided by the Spirit, we are ever to act and speak "in a new way," with renewed mind and heart.

What does this imply, so far as the ordination of women is concerned? Although Jesus never *said* anything about this, either for or against, his *actions* speak for themselves. In the words of a French Calvinist, Jean-Jacques von Allmen:

> The New Testament, in spite of the chance of total renewal which it provides for women as well as for men, never testifies that a woman could be, in a public and authorized way, representative of Christ. To no woman does Jesus say, "He who hears you, hears me." To no woman does he make the promise to ratify in heaven what she has bound or loosed on earth. To no woman does he entrust the ministry of public preach-

[9]*Commonitorium Primum* 22:27 (PL 50:667).

ing. To no woman does he give the command to baptize
or to preside at the communion of his Body and Blood.
To no woman does he commit his flock.[10]

We are confronted here by the question of our *obedience*
to Christ: are we as Christians to remain faithful to his
example or not? Do we accept the "givenness" and finality
of the revelation in Jesus Christ, and do we believe in the
apostolic character of the Church? Do we wish to belong to
the same Church as that which Christ founded? In the words
of a leading Orthodox theologian, Fr. John Meyendorff:

> The Church today claims to be "apostolic." This means
> that its faith is based upon the testimony of Christ's
> eyewitnesses, that its ministry is *Christ's* and that it is
> defined in terms of the unique, unrepeatable act of
> God, accomplished in Christ *once*. . . . No new revela-
> tion can complete or replace what Jesus Christ did
> "when the fullness of the time was come" (Gal. 4:4).
> The Gospel of Christ cannot be written anew because
> "the fullness of time" came then and not at any other
> time. There is a sense in which all Christians must
> become Christ's contemporaries. Therefore, the very
> "historical conditioning" which characterizes the Gos-
> pel of Christ is, in a sense, *normative for us*. The
> twentieth century is not an absolute norm; the apostolic
> age is.[11]

Here, then, is the first and fundamental argument that the
Orthodox Church employs. Faced by the unanimous and un-
varying practice of Christ's Church from apostolic times up
to our own, we in the twentieth century have no authority to
alter the basic patterns of Christian faith and life.

Our appeal as Orthodox is neither to scripture alone nor
to tradition alone, but to both at once.[12] We do not appeal

[10]"Is the Ordination of Women to the Pastoral Ministry Justifiable?,"
in Lutge, 35.
[11]*The Orthodox Church* (September 1975) 4.
[12]Compare the official commentary of the Sacred Congregation for the

simply to the fact that Christ chose only men to be apostles, but to the fact that for more than nineteen centuries Christ's body, the Church, has never ordained any except men to the priesthood and episcopate. Our appeal is to the total life of the Church over two thousand years—and not only to what was said but to what was done. It is, of course, true that the apostles whom Christ chose were not only males but also circumcised Jews. Almost at once, however, in the lifetime of virtually all the chief eyewitnesses of the Word, of all those who were qualified in a unique sense to share "the mind of Christ" (1 Co 2:16), the Church decreed circumcision and the other requirements of the Jewish law to be no longer binding (Ac 15:23-29). All ministries were henceforth open to Jews and Gentiles equally. But neither the apostles themselves nor their successors have admitted women to the priesthood. The difference between the two cases is immediately apparent, and it is enormous.

Our arguments against the ordination of women, then, are not based solely upon certain isolated statements in the Pauline epistles, such as 1 Corinthians 14:34-35 or 1 Timothy 2:11-12, important though these texts undoubtedly are. We appeal rather to the manner in which scriptural revelation as a whole has been interpreted, applied and lived. Scripture and tradition, here as always, are inseparable and "correlative," to use the language of the Anglican-Orthodox Agreed Statement signed at Moscow in 1976.[13] Tradition is nothing other than the *internal continuity* that exists between the New Testament and the subsequent thought and life of the Church. The ordination of women as priests is excluded precisely because it conflicts with this living continuity.

However, if this appeal to tradition is to be properly understood, three underlying presuppositions need to be rendered explicit.

Doctrine of the Faith on its decree *Inter Insigniores*: "This brings us to a fundamental observation: we must not expect the New Testament *on its own* to resolve in a clear fashion the question of the possibility of women acceding to the priesthood" (*The Ordination of Women*, CTS Do 494, p. 8).

[13]See K. Ware and C. Davey, *Anglican-Orthodox Dialogue* (London 1977) 84.

(1) Jesus Christ is not only complete man but true and perfect God. He is within history, but also above history. We do not see in him merely a human teacher, bound by the conventions of his age—he is the Word of God, from whose lips we hear not private opinions soon to grow outdated, but the eternal truth. Indeed, far from being subservient to contemporary customs, Christ often showed a striking independence. He told his disciples, "You have heard what was said by the men of old; but *I* say to you . . ." (Mt 5:21-22); he claimed to be master of the Sabbath, openly breaking the accepted regulations; he ate with tax-collectors and sinners; to the astonishment of his followers, he spoke with the Samaritan woman, and in general ignored rules normally observed by a Jewish rabbi of the time in his dealings with the female sex. Thus, if the Son of God had wanted to appoint women as apostles, he would have done so, whatever the existing conventions within Judaism or elsewhere in the ancient world. And the fact that he did not choose them as apostles must remain decisive for us today. Are we to assert that the incarnate Word and Wisdom of God was mistaken, and that we at the end of the twentieth century understand the truth better than he did?

(2) The second point is a corollary of the first. As Christ's body, as the "pillar and ground of the truth" (1 Tm 3:15), the Church is more than a fallible human association. Christ has promised: "The Spirit of truth will guide you into all truth" (Jn 16:13). Errors may arise among members of the Church, but they never finally prevail, for Christ has assured us that the truth will prove in the long run invincible. Are we to believe that this promise of Christ has failed? Are we to say that, in excluding women from the priesthood, the Church has erred for nearly two thousand years, unjustly denying to half the human race its legitimate rights?

But, so it is argued, the Church made precisely such a mistake in regard to slavery. If it took the Church eighteen centuries to recognize the evils of slavery, why should it not have taken the Church one century more to end the unjustifiable subservience of women? On closer investigation, however, the parallel proves far from exact. The distinction be-

tween male and female is part of the order of nature; that
between freemen and slaves is not. As St. Basil remarks, "No
man is a slave by nature."[14] Slavery only came into existence
subsequent to the fall. The distinction between male and
female, by contrast, existed prior to the fall and is inherent in
human nature as originally created by God (Gn 1:27). Furthermore, several fathers, most notably St. Gregory of Nyssa,
inveighed vehemently against slavery as an evil—a necessary
evil, perhaps, yet an evil nonetheless.[15] But not a single
father ever spoke of the limitation of the priesthood to men
as a necessary evil. As Fr. John Saward rightly concludes,
"The argument from the example of slavery will not stand
up to close examination."[16]

(3) On many minor details of church life, so it might be
argued, our Lord perhaps gave no specific instructions, leaving
later generations free to resolve these matters as they think
best. But—and this is our third presupposition—the admission
of women to the priesthood is not a minor detail. It vitally
affects our understanding both of priesthood and of human
nature. If women can and should be priests, then their exclusion for two millennia is a grave injustice, a tragic error. Are
we to attribute a mistake of this magnitude to the fathers and
the ecumenical councils, to the apostles and the Son of God?

An Argument from Silence?

Sometimes it is claimed that the appeal to tradition is
nothing more than an argument from absence or silence, and
therefore lacking in cogency. It is true, so the argument runs,
that there is nothing in scripture and tradition that explicitly
commands the ordination of women to the priesthood; yet
at the same time there is nothing that explicitly forbids it.

[14]*On the Holy Spirit* 20:51 (PG 32:160D). Compare John Chrysostom,
Homily 22 on Ephesians 1 (PG 62:155).
[15]*Homily 4 on Ecclesiastes* (PG 44:664C-668A; ed. Jaeger-Alexander, 334-
8).
[16]*The Case against the Ordination of Women* (London: The Church
Literature Association, 1975) 6.

The question was never seriously posed until our own day, and thus remains open.

To this it must be answered, first, that we need to listen not only to the words but to the silence of scripture and tradition. Not everything is outwardly defined. Certain doctrines, never formally defined, are yet held by the Church with an unmistakable inner conviction, an unruffled unanimity, which is just as binding as an explicit proclamation.

Secondly, it is not in fact correct to say that until our own day the matter was passed over in silence. On the contrary, it was often discussed in the early Church. The *Apostolic Church Order*, as we have seen, directly states that women are not to officiate at the eucharist. A hundred years earlier, Tertullian (d. c. 225) was equally definite: "It is not permitted for a woman to speak in church, nor yet to teach, nor to anoint, nor to make the offering, nor to claim for herself any office performed by men or any priestly ministry."[17] The *Apostolic Constitutions* (late fourth century) discuss the ministry of women in some detail, and in the same terms as Tertullian. Women are not to preach or baptize, and a fortiori it is implied that they do not celebrate the eucharist. The reason given is, specifically, faithfulness to Christ's example: he never entrusted such tasks to women, although he could easily have done so, and thus the Church has no power to commission women for work of this kind.[18]

Nor did the question of women priests remain merely hypothetical in the early history of the Church. Various schismatic groups in the second and fourth centuries had women as priests and bishops: the gnostic Marcosians, for example,[19] the Montanists[20] and the Collyridians.[21] Referring to the latter, St. Epiphanius (d. 403) examines at length the possibility of women priests. "Since the beginning of time,"

[17]*On the Veiling of Virgins* 9:1 (CC 2:1218-9).

[18]*Apostolic Constitutions* 3:6:1-2 and 3:9:4 (ed. Funk, 191, 201); cf 8:28:6 (530).

[19]Irenaeus, *Against the Heresies* 1:13:2 (ed. Harvey, 1:116-7); cf Tertullian, *The Prescription of Heretics* 41:5 (CC 1:221).

[20]Epiphanius, *Panarion* 49:2:2, 49:2:5, 49:3:2 (ed. Holl, 243-4).

[21]Ibid., 79:1:7 (ed. Holl, 476); cf 78:23:4 (473), on the Antidikomariamitae.

he states, "a woman has never served God as priest."[22] (He means, of course, in the Old Testament; he knew that there were priestesses in the pagan fertility cults.) In the New Testament, although we find female prophets (Lk 2:36; Ac 21:9), no woman is ever an apostle, bishop or presbyter. Christ had many women among his immediate followers— Mary his mother, Salome and others from Galilee, Martha and Mary the sisters of Lazarus—yet on none of them did he confer the apostolate or priesthood. "That there exists in the Church an order of deaconesses is undisputed; but they are not allowed to perform any priestly functions." Besides deaconesses, the Church also has orders of widows and old women; but we never find "female presbyters or priestesses." "After so many generations" Christians cannot now start ordaining priestesses for the first time. Such, then, is Epiphanius' conclusion concerning women and the ministerial priesthood: "God never appointed to this ministry a single woman upon earth."[23]

Most Orthodox today would find Epiphanius' treatment of the subject both convincing and sufficient. The ordination of women to the priesthood is an innovation, with no sound basis whatsoever in Holy Tradition. The evidence is explicit and unanimous, and there is nothing further to be said. It has to be admitted, however, that this argument from tradition will seem inadequate to the majority of Christians in the West, even to many who are themselves opposed to the ordination of women priests. It is not enough for them to be told *that* it is not in tradition; they wish to know *why* it is not. In the words of an Orthodox woman theologian, Mme Elisabeth Behr-Sigel: "To those who ask from us the bread of understanding, it is not enough to offer only the stones of certainties hardened by negation."[24] We need in fact to advance beyond an appeal to the external facts of tradition, and to inquire into its inner content. This will oblige us to consider the delicate subject of priesthood in its relation to sexuality—

[22]*Panarion* 79:2:3.
[23]*Panarion* 79:2:3-79:7:4 (477-82).
[24]"La femme dans l'Église orthodoxe. Vision céleste et histoire," in *Contacts* 29:4 (1977) 318.

a theme most Orthodox theologians prefer to avoid, for here it is dangerous to say too much. But then, it is also dangerous to say too little.

Royal Priesthood and Ministerial Priesthood

There are three interdependent truths which need to be kept in balance: (1) *One, and one alone, is priest*: Jesus Christ, the unique high priest of the new covenant, the "one mediator between God and men" (1 Tm 2:5), is the sole true celebrant in every sacramental act. (2) *All are priests*: by virtue of our creation in God's image and likeness, and also by virtue of the renewal of that image through baptism and anointing with chrism (western "confirmation"), we are all of us, clergy and laity together, "a royal priesthood, a holy nation" (1 Pt 2:9), set apart for God's service. (3) *Only some are priests*: certain members of the Church are set apart in a more specific way, through prayer and the laying-on of hands, to serve God in the ministerial priesthood.

It is vitally important to preserve a proper balance and distinction between the second and the third forms of priesthood, between the royal priesthood of *sanctity* and this ministerial priesthood of *order*. In many of the arguments used to support women priests, so it seems to the Orthodox, these two levels of priesthood are unhappily confused. For instance, St. Paul's words in Galatians 3:28, "There is neither male nor female, for you are all one in Christ Jesus," are often cited out of context in favor of women priests. But in fact, as the preceding sentence shows, Paul is thinking here of baptism, not ordination; this text refers to the royal priesthood of the whole people of God, not to the ministerial priesthood of order.

Women, to an equal degree with men, are created in God's image; to an equal degree with men, they are recreated in baptism and endowed with the charisms of the Holy Spirit in postbaptismal anointing. As regards the second level of priesthood, therefore, they are in every respect as much "kings and priests" (Rv 1:6) as any man can ever be. This royal priesthood consists above all in the power possessed by each human person, made according to the divine image, to act as a creator after the likeness of God the Creator. Each is able to mold and fashion the world, revealing fresh patterns and a new meaning in created things, making each material object articulate and spiritual. The royal priesthood is likewise expressed in the fact that each human person is a "eucharistic animal," capable of praising and glorifying God for the gift of the world, and so of turning each thing into a sacrament and means of communion with him. Each is capable of offering the world back to its Maker in thanksgiving, of presenting his or her own self, body and soul together, as a "living sacrifice" to the Holy Trinity (Rm 12:1).

"Thine own of thine own, we offer to thee, on behalf of all and for all" (Liturgy of St. John Chrysostom). Such is the essence of the universal priesthood inherent in all human nature. In terms of this hieratic self-offering, both man and woman are equally priests of the created universe, by virtue of the common humanity that they share. At the same time, each exercises this priesthood in a distinct way, for the differences of sexuality extend deep into our human nature and are by no means restricted to the act of procreation.

The human person who expresses most perfectly this royal and universal priesthood is not in fact a man but a woman—the Blessed Virgin Mary. She is the supreme example not just of female sanctity but of human sanctity as such. In the words of G.K. Chesterton, "Men are men, but Man is a woman." "Behold, the handmaid of the Lord" (Lk 1:38). At the annunciation, as throughout her life, the Mother of God exemplifies that priestly act of self-offering which is the true vocation of us all. This point has been well emphasized by the head of the Greek Orthodox Church in Britain, Archbishop Athenagoras of Thyateira: "God in his love sent his Son to be a man, whilst in return humanity offered Saint Mary the Virgin to be the cleansed and perfected vessel in which humanity and divinity meet in the God-manhood of Christ."[25]

[25]"The Question of the Ordination of Women," in *The Orthodox Herald*, no. 125-6 (May-June 1975) 14.

It is significant that the movement for the ordination of women should first have emerged in those Christian communities that tend to neglect the Holy Virgin's place in Christ's redemptive work. "There is no doubt in my mind," says Fr. John Meyendorff, "that the Protestant rejection of the veneration of Mary and its various consequences (such as, for example, the really 'male-dominated' Protestant worship, deprived of sentiment, poetry and intuitive mystery-perception) is one of the *psychological* reasons which explains the recent emergence of institutional feminism."[26]

The example of the Mother of God shows us how important it is to differentiate between the second level of priesthood and the third. She—in whose person we see perfectly expressed the royal priesthood of the Christian believer—was never a priest in the ministerial sense. Speaking on the level of the royal priesthood of self-offering, the *Apostolic Constitutions* are able to affirm, "Let the widow realize that she is the altar of God."[27] But the very same passage excludes the possibility that the widows, or any other women, could act as ministerial priests.

Two points about the ministerial priesthood need to be underlined. First, the ministry is not to be envisaged in "professional" terms, as a "job" that a woman can carry out as competently as a man, and which she has an equal "right" to perform. Still less is the ministry to be conceived in terms of power and domination, as a "privilege" from which woman is being unjustly excluded. "It shall not be so among you" (Mt 20:26). The Church is not a power structure or a business enterprise, but the body of Christ; the ministerial priesthood is not a human invention devised for purposes of efficiency, but a gift of God's grace. Far from being a "right" or "privilege," the ministry is a call to service, and this call comes from God. In the Church, all is gift, all is grace. When a man is called to the ministerial priesthood, this is invariably a gift of grace from God, never a "right."

Secondly, the ministerial priest is not to be seen in secular and pseudo-democratic terms, as a deputy or representative

[26]*The Orthodox Church* (September 1975) 4.
[27]*Apostolic Constitutions* 3:6:3 (ed. Funk, 191).

merely exercising by delegation the royal priesthood that belongs to the Christian people as a whole. On the contrary, the ministerial priest derives his priesthood not by delegation from the people, but immediately from Christ. As Justin the Martyr (d. c. 165) affirms, "The twelve apostles depend upon the power of Christ the eternal priest,"[28] and the same is true of their successors the bishops. The royal priesthood and the ministerial priesthood are *both* ways of sharing *directly* in the priesthood of Christ, and neither is derived by devolution through the other.

The Priest as Icon

But why, we ask, should the ministerial priesthood be limited to men, whereas the royal priesthood is conferred on all alike? Why should God not call women to be priests? The answer lies in the "iconic" character of the ministerial priesthood. In the prayer before the Great Entrance (the offertory procession) at the Divine Liturgy, the priest addresses these words to Christ: "Thou art he who offers and he who is offered." It is Christ himself who makes the eucharistic offering. As the deacon states at the very beginning of the service, "It is time for the Lord to act." "Our Lord and God Jesus Christ," says St. Cyprian of Carthage (d. 258), "is himself the high priest of God the Father; he offered himself as a sacrifice to the Father and commanded that this should be done in memory of him; thus, the priest truly acts in the place of Christ [*vice Christi*]."[29] "It is the Father, the Son and the Holy Spirit who perform everything," teaches St. John Chrysostom (d. 407); "but the priest lends his tongue and supplies his hand."[30] "It is not man who causes the bread and wine to become Christ's body and blood: this is done by Christ himself, crucified for our sakes. The priest stands before us, doing what Christ did and speaking the words that he spoke; but the power and grace are from God."[31]

[28]*Dialogue with Trypho* 42:1 (ed. Otto, 140).
[29]*Letter* 63 14 (ed. Hartel, 713).
[30]*Homily 77 on John* 4 (PG 59:472).
[31]*On the Treachery of Judas* 1:6 (PG 49:380). Cf the *Commentary on*

The priesthood, then, is always Christ's and not ours. The priest in church is not "another" priest alongside Christ, and the sacrifice that he offers, in union with the people, is not "another" sacrifice, but always Christ's own. The ministerial priest, as priest, possesses no identity of his own: his priesthood exists solely in order to make Christ present. This understanding of the ministerial priesthood is clearly affirmed by St. Paul: "We come therefore as Christ's ambassadors; it is as if God were appealing to you through us" (2 Co 5:20); "you welcomed me as an angel of God, even as Christ Jesus" (Ga 4:14). St. Ignatius of Antioch (d. c. 107) speaks similarly: "The bishop presides as the image of God."[32] In the words of Antiochus the Monk (seventh century): "The priests should be imitators of their high priest [i.e., the bishop], and he in his turn should be an imitator of Christ the high priest."[33] In the consecration service of an Orthodox bishop, the chief officiant prays: "O Christ our God . . . who hast appointed for us teachers to occupy thy throne . . . make this man to be an imitator of thee the true Shepherd."

The bishop or priest is therefore an imitator, image or sign of Christ the one mediator and high priest. In short, the ministerial priest is an icon. "Standing between God and men," writes St. Theodore the Studite (d. 826), "the priest in the priestly invocations is an imitation of Christ. For the Apostle says: 'There is one God, and one mediator between God and men, the man Christ Jesus' [1 Tm 2:5]. Thus, the priest is an icon of Christ."[34]

This notion of the priest as an icon has far-reaching implications. First of all, there can be no question of any identification between the priest and Christ, for an icon is in no sense identical with that which it depicts.[35]

Secondly, an icon is not the same as a photograph or a realistic portrait; and so, when the priest is considered as an

Galatians 3:28 (PG 61:663), on the sacrament of baptism: "the words of God are spoken through the priest" (not by him).
[32]To the Magnesians 6:1; cf To the Trallians 3:1; To the Smyrneans 8:1.
[33]Homily 123 (PG 89:1817C).
[34]Seven Chapters against the Iconoclasts 4 (PG 99:493C); cf Theodore, Letter 1 11 (PG 99:945C).
[35]Cf Ware and Davey, Anglican-Orthodox Dialogue, 74.

icon, this is not to be understood grossly, in a literal or naturalistic sense. The priest is not an actor on the stage, "made up" to look like Christ.

Thirdly, according to the principle enunciated by St. Basil and used in the iconoclast controversy, "The honor shown to the icon is referred to the prototype."[36] When we venerate the icon of the Savior, we do not honor wood and paint, but through wood and paint we honor Christ himself. The same is true of the priest as an icon. He is not honored in and for himself—all the honor is referred to Christ. In terming the priest an icon, we do not thereby attribute to him any special kind of intrinsic personal sanctity; we do not set him, as a human being, on a higher level than others. The greatest in the kingdom of heaven are not the clergy but the saints. Here, as always, a careful distinction must be made between royal priesthood and ministerial priesthood, between the personal priesthood of sanctity and the iconic priesthood of order.

Fourthly, it is the function of an icon to *make present* a spiritual reality that surpasses it, but of which it acts as the sign. As an icon of Christ, therefore, the priest is not just a deputy or legal delegate of the people, and neither is he the vicar or surrogate of an *absent* Christ. The purpose of an icon is not to remind us of someone who is absent but to *render that person present.* Christ and his saints are present as active participants in the liturgy through their icons in the church; and Christ is likewise present in the liturgy through his icon the priest.

Fifthly and finally, as an icon of the unique high priest Christ, the ministerial priest must be male. In the words of Fr. Alexander Schmemann, "If the bearer, the icon and the fulfiller of that unique priesthood, is *man* and not woman, it is because Christ is *man* and not woman."[37] "For the Eastern Orthodox," writes Fr. Maximos Aghiorgoussis, "it is imperative to preserve the symbolic correspondence between Christ as a male and the ordained priest. . . . The ordination of

---

[36]*On the Holy Spirit* 18:45 (PG 32:149C). Basil is speaking here about trinitarian relationships, not about iconography; but in the disputes of the eighth and ninth centuries his words were applied to the holy icons (see John of Damascus, *On the Holy Icons* 1:21; ed. Kotter, 108).

[37]"Concerning Women's Ordination," in Lutge, 14-5.

women to the Holy Priesthood is untenable since it would
disregard the symbolic and iconic value of male priesthood,
both as representing Christ's malehood and the fatherly role
of the Father in the Trinity, by allowing female persons to
interchange with male persons a role which cannot be inter-
changed."[38]

There are two points implicit in these words of Fr. Maximos. First, he speaks not only of Christ's "manhood" but of
his "malehood." At his human birth, Christ not only became
man in the sense of becoming human (ἄνθρωπος, *homo*),
but he also became man in the sense of becoming male
(ἀνήρ, *vir*). Certainly Christ is the Savior of all humankind,
of men and women equally; at his incarnation he took up into
himself and healed our common humanity. But at the same
time, we should keep in view the *particularity* of the incarnation. Christ was born at a specific time and place, from a
specific mother. He did not become human just in an abstract
or generalized sense—he became a particular human being. As
such, he could not be both a male and a female at once, and
he was in fact a male.

Secondly, men and women are not interchangeable, like
counters or identical machines. The difference between them,
as we have already insisted, extends far more deeply than
the physical act of procreation. The sexuality of human beings
is not an accident, but affects them in their very identity and
in their deepest mystery. Unlike the differentiation between
Jew and Greek or between slave and free—which reflects
man's fallen state and is due to social convention, not to
nature—the differentiation between male and female is an
aspect of humanity's natural state before the fall. The life of
grace in the Church is not bound by social conventions or
the conditions produced by the fall. But it does conform to
the order of nature, in the sense of unfallen nature as created
by God. Thus, the distinction between male and female is
not abolished in the Church.

We are not saved *from* our masculinity and femininity, but
in them; and to say otherwise is to be gnostic or Marcionite.

[38]*Women Priests?* (Brookline, Mass.: Holy Cross Orthodox Press, 1976)
3, 5.

We cannot repent of being male and female, but only of the way in which we are these things. Grace cooperates with nature and builds upon it; the Church's task is to sanctify the natural order, not to repudiate it. In the Church we are male and female, not sexless. Dedicated virginity within the church community is not the rejection of sex, but a way of consecrating it. In the words of Fr. Meyendorff, "The Christian faith, as held by the Church, is not a negation of nature but its salvation. The 'new creation' does not suppress the 'old,' but renews and transfigures it."[39] He goes on to quote the words of an Orthodox statement at an Anglican-Orthodox consultation held in America in 1974: "God created men as 'male and female,' establishing a diversity of functions and gifts; these functions and gifts are complementary but not at all interchangeable. . . . There is every reason for Christians to oppose the current trends which tend to make men and women interchangeable in their functions and roles, and thus lead to the dehumanization of life." C.S. Lewis saw this danger many years ago: "As the State grows more like a hive or an anthill it needs an increasing number of workers who can be treated as neuters. This may be inevitable for our secular life. But in our Christian life we must return to reality."[40]

Such, then, is the Orthodox understanding of the ministerial priesthood. The priest is an icon of Christ; and since the incarnate Christ became not only man but a male—since, furthermore, in the order of nature the roles of male and female are not interchangeable—it is necessary that the priest should be male. Those Western Christians who do not in fact regard the priest as an icon of Christ are of course free to ordain women as ministers. They are not, however, creating women priests, but dispensing with priesthood altogether.

[39]*The Orthodox Church* (September 1975) 4.
[40]"Priestesses in the Church?," from *God in the Dock*, ed. W. Hooper (Grand Rapids, Mich.: Eerdmans, 1970) 238 (from an article originally published in 1948).

The Value of Symbols

Some will remain unconvinced by this argument from the iconic character of the priesthood, because it involves an appeal to symbolism. "Do not offer us symbols," they will object, "but give us proof, based on logical reasoning." In answer, it must be at once admitted that the rightness of our symbols is not something that can be logically demonstrated. A symbol can be verified, lived, prayed—but not "proved." Church life, however, is not to be reduced to Euclidean geometry; while our reasoning powers should be employed to the full, we cannot grasp spiritual truth exclusively through syllogisms. Symbols and archetypes provide a vital key for the comprehension of literature and art, and they are no less important in religious faith and prayer. A symbol has the advantage of being far easier to understand than a verbal explanation, while at the same time conveying truths too profound to be formulated in words. In worship, as in family life, there is a "deep symbolism of actions and things,"[41] reaching down to the hidden roots of our being. If this symbolism is ignored or outraged, our relationship with both God and with other humans alike will be fatally impoverished.

In our subconscious there are certain symbols and archetypes that are not invented but *given*. The same is true of the symbols revealed in Holy Scripture and used in Christian worship. We cannot "prove" these symbols; all we know is that God has set his seal upon certain images and not upon others. We have been taught to say "Our Father who art in heaven," and not "Our Mother who art in heaven"; the second person of the Holy Trinity is God the Son, not God the Daughter; Christ is the new Adam, not the new Eve; he is the Bridegroom and the Church is his bride—the relationship cannot be reversed. These symbols are "given," and they are absolutely fundamental.

Needless to say, our symbolic theology must be balanced by the use of apophatic or negative theology. God in himself is neither masculine nor feminine, since he infinitely trans-

---

[41] I take this phrase from the decree *Inter Insigniores* (CTS Do 494, p. 11).

cends any such categories. Yet it does not therefore follow
that we are free to apply to him whatever symbols we please.
On the contrary, if we were to substitute a Mother Goddess
for God the Father, we would not simply be altering a piece
of incidental imagery—but we would be replacing Christianity
with a new kind of religion.[42] The male character of the
Christian priesthood forms an integral element in this pattern
of revealed, God-given symbolism, which is not to be tampered with. Christ is the Bridegroom and the Church is his
bride. And how can the living icon of the Bridegroom be
other than a man?

Diversities of Gifts

If our conclusion thus far has a negative appearance, this
is because the wrong question was posed in the first place.
Rather than ask, "can women be priests?" we ought to be
asking, "what are the distinctive gifts conferred by God on
women, and how can these gifts be expressed in the Church's
ministry?" Instead of trying to ordain women as priests,
Christians today need to explore and develop the special
forms of service in the Church that women are best able to
perform. The question is not "do women have a role of leadership in the Church?" but "what is the nature of that role?"

It is one of the chief glories of human nature that men
and women, although equal, are not interchangeable. Together
they exercise a common ministry that neither could exercise
alone; for within that shared ministry each has a particular
role. There exists between them a certain order or hierarchy,
with man as the "head" and woman as the partner or "helper"
(Gn 2:18), and yet this differentiation does not imply any
fundamental inequality between them. Within the Trinity,
God the Father is the source and "head" of Christ (1 Co
11:3), and yet the three persons are essentially equal. The
same is true of the relationship between man and woman.

---

[42]Very occasionally in the Christian tradition, feminine imagery has been
applied to the deity, in particular to the Holy Spirit (see below, note 60).
But this is the exception; all the main symbols "given" to us are masculine.

The Greek fathers, although often negative in their opinion
of the female sex, were on the whole absolutely clear about
the basic human equality of man and woman: both alike are
created in God's image. The subordination of woman to man
and her exploitation do not reflect the order of nature created
by God, but the contranatural conditions resulting from
original sin.[43] Equal yet different according to the order of
nature, man and woman complete each other through their
free cooperation. And this complementarity is to be respected
on every level—when at home in the circle of the family,
when out at work, and not least in the life of the Church,
which blesses and transforms the natural order while not
obliterating it.

Much current propaganda for the ordination of women
priests seems to envisage the priesthood as virtually the only
possible form of ministry in the Church. It is assumed that,
because women are not allowed to be priests, they are in
consequence left with no proper role to play in church life.
The diversity of ministries—such as we find, for example, in
the *Apostolic Church Order*—is all too often overlooked. The
present campaign for women priests may thus be seen as "the
bitter fruit of the clericalization of the Church,"[44] "a typically
western and medieval form of clericalism."[45] Women are
being wrongly led to seek priestly ordination because other
forms of ecclesial service have been neglected. But this point
has a relevance for men as well: often men assume that, if
they "have a vocation," it must be to the priesthood, because
they do not think in terms of any other type of ministry. We
need to recover the full Pauline vision of the Church as unity
in diversity.

Among the Orthodox thinkers who in the recent past
have written about the distinctive gifts and ministry of women

[43]See, for example, Clement of Alexandria, *Stromateis* 4:8 (ed. Staehlin,
275, 21ff); John Chrysostom, *Sermon 2* 2 and *Sermon 4* 1 *on Genesis* (PG
54:589, 593-4); *Homily 26 on 1 Corinthians* 2 (PG 61:214-5); Ps.-Gregory
of Nyssa, *On the Creation of Man* (PG 44:276A; ed. Hörner, 34, 8ff); Basil
of Seleucia, *Oration 2* (PG 85:44A); Procopius of Gaza, *On Genesis 2:18*
(PG 87(1):172A).
[44]O. Clément, *Questions sur l'homme* (Paris 1972) 119.
[45]Fr. John Meyendorff, in *The Orthodox Church* (September 1975) 4.

are Nicholas Berdyaev, Fr. Lev Gillet, Olivier Clément and, above all, Paul Evdokimov.[46] Their views have been carefully summarized in a recent article by Mme Behr-Sigel, who wisely warns against the danger of thinking in terms of "cultural stereotypes."[47] Certainly, the whole subject requires much more thorough investigation on the Orthodox part. We need to hear the voice not only of the male theologians but of the Orthodox women themselves. An encouraging start—but no more than a start—was made by the Consultation of Orthodox Women, held at Agapia, Romania, on September 11-17, 1976.[48]

Brief mention may be made of four among the ministries that Orthodox women are, or could be, fulfilling.

(1) Although in the New Testament no woman was chosen to be an apostle, the Orthodox Church recognizes a number of women as ἰσαπόστολος, "equal to the apostles." Among them are, for instance, St. Mary Magdalene; the martyr Thekla; St. Helena, mother of the Emperor Constantine; and St. Nina, the missionary who converted Georgia.

(2) Women "equal to the apostles," acting as preachers and missionaries, have never been common in the past. But there is a more hidden form of ministry that Orthodox women have never ceased to perform: that of the *priest's wife.* Within Orthodoxy the parish priest is in principle always a married man. If for special reasons a parish is put in charge of a monk or a celibate priest (there are in fact extremely few unmarried clergy who are not in monastic vows), it is definitely to be regarded as an exception to the standard rule. The fact that the parish priest has a wife is not to be seen as merely accidental or peripheral to his pastoral work;

[46]See Berdyaev, "The New Middle Ages," in *The End of Our Time* (London 1933) 117-8; Un Moine de l'Eglise d'Orient [Gillet], *Amour sans limites* (Chevetogne 1971) 96; Clément, *Questions sur l'homme,* 114-21 (brief, but highly perceptive); and Evdokimov's important study *La femme et le salut du monde. Etude d'anthropologie chrétienne sur les charismes du femme* (Tournai/Paris 1958)—not yet (alas) translated into English, and long since unobtainable in the French original.

[47]"La femme dans l'Eglise orthodoxe," 303-9.

[48]See the report *Orthodox Women: Their Role and Participation in the Orthodox Church,* published by the World Council of Churches, Sub-Unit on Women in Church and Society (Geneva 1977).

nor should the priest's wife merely be someone who happens to have married a future clergyman. Her status in the parish is indicated by her title: in the Greek Church the priest is called *presbyteros* or *pappas,* and his wife *presbytera* or *pappadia;* in the Russian Church the priest is "little father" (*batushka*), and his wife is "little mother" (*matushka*). If the woman in the home acts as giver and protector of life, the priest's wife is called to do this throughout the parish. Just as the priest is father not to his own children alone but to the entire community, so the priest's wife is called to be mother alike in her own family and in the parochial family as a whole. Yet she is not ordained for this task, but is simply exercising in a particular manner the royal priesthood that is the common inheritance of all. Her maternal vocation has to be exercised with the utmost discretion, not so much through anything she *says* or *does,* as through what she *is.*

(3) There is, however, one form of the ordained ministry to which women are certainly called, and that is the ministry of *deaconesses.* The members of the Agapia Consultation pleaded for a "reactivation" of this ancient order, which in the Orthodox Church has fallen into disuse since the twelfth century. They spoke of the ministry of the deaconess as a "life-time commitment to full vocational service in the Church . . . an extension of the sacramental life of the Church into the life of society."[49] Already in the Russian Church before the 1917 revolution there were several schemes for a full restoration of the order of deaconesses, although in the end nothing was done.[50] And since 1952 the Church of Greece has had a School for Deaconesses—the present building was opened in 1957—though the members are not actually ordained. I am told, however, that ordained deaconesses exist within the Coptic Church of Egypt.

There is a difference of opinion among contemporary Orthodox as to the exact status of deaconesses in the early Church. Some regard them as essentially a "lay" and not an

[49]*Orthodox Women,* 50.
[50]See Fr. Sergei Hackel, "Mother Maria Skobtsova: Deaconess Manquée?" in *Eastern Churches Review* 1 (1967) 264-6.

"ordained" ministry.[51] But others point out that the liturgical rite for the laying-on of hands received by deaconesses is exactly parallel to that for deacons—which implies that deaconesses receive, as do deacons, a genuine sacramental ordination: not just a χειροθεσία but a χειροτονία.[52] All Orthodox are agreed, however, that there is a sharp distinction between the diaconate and the priesthood. The deacon, and a fortiori the deaconess, does not perform the consecration at the eucharist, does not bless the people and in general does not act as a liturgical icon of Christ. There is a special funeral office for priests, but when a deacon dies the burial service is the same as that for a layman. The existence of deaconesses within the Church is thus in no sense a justification for women priests. As the Agapia Consultation insisted, "The office of deaconess is distinct and not new, nor can it be considered as a 'first step' to the ordained priesthood."[53]

In the *Teaching of the Apostles,* a Syriac work of the early third century, it is suggested that the deacon has a special link with the second person of the Holy Trinity, and the deaconess with the third person: "The deacon stands in the place of Christ; and do you love him. And the deaconess shall be honoured by you in the place of the Holy Spirit."[54] The implications of this idea have been developed, in a fascinating but somewhat speculative manner, by Paul Evdokimov;[55] a similar line of thought can be found in an article

[51]This is the view of the Romanian theologian Prof. Nicolae Chitescu; see his article in the World Council of Churches pamphlet *Concerning the Ordination of Women* (Geneva 1964).

[52]See the article by Prof. Evangelos Theodorou of Athens University, "The Ministry of Deaconesses in the Greek Orthodox Church," in *Orthodox Women,* 37-43; also Militsa Zernov, "Women's Ministry in the Church," in *Eastern Churches Review* 7 (1975) 34-9.

Prof. Panagiotis Trempelas considers that deaconesses in the early Church "received, not just a laying-on of hands (χειροθεσία) but a real ordination (χειροτονία), being placed on a level somewhat lower than the deacon, but higher than the subdeacon." Δογματικὴ τῆς ᾿Ορθοδόξου Καθολικῆς ᾿Εκκλησίας 3 (Athens 1961) 291-2; French trans. by P. Dumont, *Dogmatique de l'Eglise orthodoxe catholique* 3 (Chevetogne 1968) 309.

[53]*Orthodox Women,* 50.

[54]*Didascalia Apostolorum,* ed. R.H. Connolly (Oxford 1929) 25 (p. 88); cf *Apostolic Constitutions* 2:26:5-6 (ed. Funk, 105).

[55]"Les charismes de la femme," in *La nouveauté de l'Esprit,* Spiritualité

by Fr. Thomas Hopko.[56] While it would be unwise to base
too much on this one passage from the *Teaching of the
Apostles* taken in isolation, we certainly have here a theme
to be explored more fully when considering the charisms of
woman. In early Syriac sources, and very occasionally in the
Greek tradition, the Holy Spirit is pictured in feminine
symbolism: the Syriac author Aphrahat (early fourth century),
for example, speaks of the Christian's relationship with "God
his Father and the Holy Spirit his Mother."[57] If man serves
in a special way as an icon of the Savior, has not woman a
distinctive role as an icon of the Paraclete?

(4) Much has been said in recent years about the importance in the Orthodox tradition of the spiritual father, of the
charismatic "abba" or "elder," styled γέρων by the Greeks
and *starets* by the Russians. But is there not a place also for
spiritual motherhood? The role of spiritual guide is closely
linked to the gifts of intercession and prophecy. And these,
as we noted at the outset, are in a special sense the charisms
of woman.

The idea of spiritual motherhood, after all, is not new.
In the *Gerontikon* or "Sayings of the Desert Fathers," alongside some 127 spiritual fathers there are three "ammas" or
spiritual mothers—Theodora, Sarah and Synkletika—and these
"ammas," although in a minority, are set upon an equal foot-
ing with the great "abbas" such as Antony, Arsenios or
Poemen. The monk Isaias, around the year 1200, even com-
piled a *Meterikon* or collection of the "Sayings of the

Orientale, 20 (Bellefontaine 1977) 245-8; cf *La femme et le salut du monde*,
16, 211.

[56]"On the Male Character of Christian Priesthood," originally published
in *St. Vladimir's Theological Quarterly* 19:3 (1975) 155-6; reprinted below
(see pp. 104-7).

[57]*On Virginity against the Jews* 18:10 (ed. Parisot, col. 839). Cf also
The Gospel according to the Hebrews, in M.R. James, *The Apocryphal New
Testament* (Oxford 1924) 2; *The Acts of Thomas* 7, 27, 39, 50 (James,
368, 376, 384, 388); Gregory of Nyssa, *Commentary on the Song of Songs*,
Sermon 6 and *Sermon 15* (ed. Langerbeck, 183, 468); Macarius, *Homily 28*
4 (ed. Dörries, 233), etc. In the West, "Mother language" is applied to God
by Julian of Norwich. These passages should not be overemphasized. In Syria,
after the middle of the fourth century, references to the Spirit as Mother
become very rare; in the Greek tradition, such references are always exceptional.

Mothers," parallel to the *Paterikon* or "Sayings of the Fathers."[58]

There is no lack of material for such a work. Indeed, in the history of monasticism it was the women who acted as pioneers rather than the men. It is customary to treat St. Antony of Egypt as the father of Christian monasticism. Yet we read that, when he first decided to give up his possessions and to embrace the ascetic way, he entrusted his younger sister to the care of a παρθενών, a "convent" of virgins.[59] Long before Antony had settled in the desert as a hermit, and long before his younger contemporary Pachomius had established the first cenobitic monasteries for men, fully organized communities for women were already in existence.

The *starets* or spiritual father in the Christian East, while commonly a priest-monk, is not always in priestly orders: the great Antony himself, like most of the early desert fathers, was never ordained. From this it is clear that the ministry of spiritual direction, although linked closely to the ministerial priesthood of order, is basically an expression of the royal priesthood of sanctity. It is therefore a calling that can be exercised by lay men—and if by lay men, then equally, yet in a different way, by lay women. In the Anglican Church, Evelyn Underhill (1875-1941) forms a notable instance of a lay woman invested with this ministry.[60] If the order of deaconesses were revived in Orthodoxy, no doubt many of them would act as spiritual mothers. Still, the role of motherhood in Christ should not be limited to them or to any other specific form of the ordained ministry.

Throughout the contemporary Christian world there is a thirst for spiritual guidance, and at the same time a severe dearth of persons blessed by the Holy Spirit to serve as guides.

[58]As yet unpublished in Greek, this *Meterikon* was translated into Russian by Bishop Feofan the Recluse and published in at least three editions. See I. Hausherr, *Direction spirituelle en Orient autrefois,* Orientalia Christiana Analecta, 144 (Rome 1955) 267.

[59]Athanasius, *Life of Antony* 3. In terming Antony the "father of monasticism," one should not forget Syria!

[60]Incidentally, she did not favor giving the priesthood to women. See her essay, "The Ideals of the Ministry of Women," in *Mixed Pastures* (London 1933); cited by V.A. Demant in *Why the Christian Priesthood is Male,* 2d ed. (London: The Church Literature Association, 1977) 20-1.

It is disappointing that in such a situation very little thought is being given to the cultivation of spiritual motherhood. The unhappy controversy about women priests is distracting our thought from the real questions.

The above, then, are four ways in which the ministry of women exists or might be further developed in the Orthodox Church today. Many more examples could of course be given, but enough has, I hope, been said to indicate how rich are the possibilities. In conclusion, let us simply end with two pictures, the first from Greece and the second from Russia.

Often in his writings, Alexander Papadiamantis (1851-1911) describes the characteristic festivals held in remote chapels in the Greek countryside. Without the participation of the women, these festivals could scarcely be held. It is they who "prepare and constitute the physical flesh for the cosmic liturgy."[61] They bake the loaves for the eucharist; they bring with them the wine and oil, the incense and the candles; they decorate the church and do the singing at the service. Without them the celebration could not take place, just as it could not take place without the priest. Here, in the offering of the eucharist, man and woman are seen cooperating together, and the role of each is essential.

Alexander Solzhenitsyn speaks likewise of the role of women in his piece "The Easter Procession." Surrounded by hostile, jeering crowds, the paschal procession makes its way round the outside of the patriarchal cathedral in Moscow at Easter midnight. First come two laymen, clearing the way; then follows the churchwarden, carrying a lantern on a pole, "glancing from side to side with apprehension"; and after him come two other men with a banner, also "huddling together from fear." At the end of the little procession come the priests and deacons, and they too, in their fear, are "bunched together, walking out of step," hurrying by as quickly as they can. But between the banner and the clergy come the women, ten of them, walking in pairs, holding thick, lighted candles. They have a tranquility that the men

---

[61]I borrow this phrase from Prof. Christos Yannaras, to whom I owe the ideas in this paragraph.

lack: ". . . elderly women with faces set in an unworldly gaze, prepared for death if they are attacked. Two out of the ten are young girls, with pure, bright faces. . . . The ten women, walking in close formation, are singing and looking as solemn as though the people round them were crossing themselves, praying and falling on their knees in repentance. They do not breathe the cigarette smoke; their ears are deaf to the vile language; the soles of their feet do not feel how the church-yard has been turned into a dance-floor."[62]

These ten, walking in the Easter procession, exemplify the women of Russia who, far more than the men, have through their courage kept alive the faith during sixty years of persecution. They prove to us that in God's Church woman is called to be not passive, not subordinate, but resolute and creative, as the Virgin Mary was at the annunciation.

[62]*Matryona's House and Other Stories*, tr. M. Glenny (Harmondsworth, Eng.: Penguin Books, 1975) 106-7.

Women and the Priestly Office According to the Scriptures

By Georges Barrois*

The subject is one of burning actuality. What is the specific function of women in the life and worship of the Church? To put it bluntly, how shall we answer the question whether women should be ordained to the priesthood, according to the meaning of "priesthood" in the biblical tradition of the Old and New Testaments? The epistle to the Hebrews recognizes Christ, the new Adam, as the eternal priest according to the order of Melchizedek. Now, does the Theotokos, the new Eve, share in the priesthood of her son, and in what measure? The Old Testament priesthood was a figure of the Christian priesthood, and both the type and its realization derive all their substance from the person and the historic work of Christ; only in relation to the latter can we ascertain the part of women in the ongoing economy of salvation in and through the Church.

The search for a definition of the religious status of women in the Judeo-Christian religion is made singularly difficult today, as it takes place in an atmosphere disturbed by stormy discussions on sexuality and an obsessive concern about the place of the woman in modern society. It amounts

*Georges A. Barrois, Professor Emeritus of Old Testament at St. Vladimir's Seminary, is now retired and living in Princeton, where he taught Scripture for many years at the Divinity School. His latest works include *The Face of Christ in the Old Testament* and *Jesus Christ and the Temple,* both published by SVS Press. "Women and the Priestly Office according to the Scriptures" was originally published in *St. Vladimir's Theological Quarterly* 19:3 (1975) 174-92.

often to passionate protests, diversely justified, as vocal as the protests of the Athenian women in the plays of Aristophanes, but without the healthy truculence.

As a matter of fact, a certain discrimination against the "devout female sex"—quoting from the Latin liturgy—cannot be denied, if we scan the documentary evidence available to us through biblical and historical data. It may indeed, however, be more apparent than real, especially if we consider the problem as a whole, and not from the narrow angle from which it is too often examined and which distorts the vision. We should read in its proper context the Synagogue's blessing at the daily morning service: "Blessed art thou, Adonaï Elohênu, king of the universe, in that thou hast not made me a woman,"[1] for which women substitute the following: "Blessed art thou . . . in that thou hast made me according to thy will." Nor should we read out of context or without the necessary exegesis the precept of the Apostle: "Let your women keep silence in the churches" (1 Co 14:34 KJV), which, quoted in Latin, has been turned into a biting irony: *taceat mulier in ecclesia.*[2]

The views taken in our days by churches and other ecclesial bodies with respect to the ordination of women vary greatly, inasmuch as they are not in agreement on the essential meaning and significance of the ministerial order. There is not much of a problem as far as most Protestant denominations are concerned, especially those of the Evangelical variety (Baptist, Methodist, and the like). The focus was shifted from the altar to the pulpit. Sacraments were, in fact, demoted to a secondary rank in popular estimation and practice, and a number of Protestant theologians gradually came to regard them as mere "audio-visual aids," useful to the faith for their power of suggestion, not for their sacral substance. This sacramental minimalism, which originated among the left-wing sixteenth-century reformationists, gained momentum

---

[1]No humor intended—simply the belief that some day a male Israelite would be manifested as the Messiah. By the same token, every Israelite woman could have hope of being chosen by God as the prospective mother of the Messiah.

[2]The Vulgate, like the Greek, reads in the plural: *mulieres in ecclesiis taceant.*

during the so-called Age of Enlightenment, and still prevails in most contemporary churches and sects, which concentrate, some of them exclusively, on preaching, teaching, counseling and social action.[3] Accordingly, the theological concept of the ministerial priesthood was reduced in fact to that of a "commissioned worker," and if ordination to the priesthood is made synonymous with appointment to a church office, then it is difficult to see why properly qualified women could not be inducted into such an office, with or without tenure! It is true that some judicatories of Protestant churches, especially on the European continent, were and still are extremely cautious with regard to the ordination of women and reluctant to install them as pastors or entrust them with a pulpit or with the celebration of the Lord's Supper. There is here an obvious inconsistency, which can be justified only if such ostracism is motivated not by way of principle, but temporarily, with regard to local conditions or the feelings of a congregation slow to accept changes and adopt new ways. Human nature being what it is, a certain amount of "male chauvinism" may be expected in these matters, even when it is theoretically reproved.

The nominalism that affects the sacramental theology and the ecclesiastical ordinances of Anglicanism and amounts in some instances to a cultured ambiguity, doubtfully supported by the branch theory and the notion of comprehensiveness, makes it extremely difficult to define clearly the position taken by the Church of England and some of her daughter or sister churches on the ordination of women to the priesthood. In the first place, what is meant here by "priesthood"? Is it the ministry as it was "protestantized" in the time of the break from Rome while retaining the hierarchical organization of the Catholic Church? Or is it the priesthood as tentatively rehabilitated to bring it back to some degree of conformity, at least in externals and to a measure in spirit, with the traditional priesthood of the Orthodox and Roman communions? Or is the term used in a mere descriptive sense, without in-

[3]Symptoms of a reversal of these trends can be observed in our days, perhaps as the by-product of ecumenical conversations, or because individual Protestants feel that they are missing an essential element of Christian life.

sistence on its theological content? On the specific problem of the ordination of women, the Anglican hierarchy has generally pronounced itself for the negative, to the dismay of militant feminists. It is not altogether clear, however, whether the bishops did so on dogmatic grounds or out of respect for what has been the age-old practice of the Church, and whether they considered their decision as eventually negotiable. A few women, braving the official interdiction, found bishops willing to ordain them, and weekly magazines printed pictures of the avant-garde priestesses in full eucharistic vestments. Whether or not women so "ordained" will be authorized to exercise their "priesthood," especially with regard to the eucharist, remains to be seen.[4] At any rate, decisions by ecclesiastical courts, while making precedents, will not necessarily solve the basic problem, which is theological in nature, not juridical.

These novelties have not yet been seen in the Roman Catholic Church, nor are they expected to happen in any foreseeable future, but the pressure of "women's lib" and the reckless theorizing of far-out scholars has prompted the hierarchy to appoint commissions of theologians and canonists to study the problem, rather than uttering a blunt *non licet*. Neither is the Orthodox policy likely to be reversed. It remains that the problem is worthy of careful examination in order to determine on which grounds ministerial priesthood must be conferred on men only. The grounds are complex, and the solution of the problem depends on a number of factors diversely interrelated, but none of which is determining with finality. Cultural factors admit of a certain (limited) plasticity and belong in tradition without having its normative authority; historical and social factors are subject to temporal and geographical conditioning; biological factors are the most permanent of all; and theological factors are rooted in the revealed dogma.

A warning is in order at this point. Simplified views of the changing status of women from early biblical times onward have been offered repeatedly, so often in fact that we have some trouble in approaching our problem from *tabula rasa*.

---

[4][Editor's note: As this article was written in 1975, it does not take into account all the recent developments in this area.]

It has been argued that Old Testament women shared in the assumed condition of inferiority of the woman in the ancient Near East and were gradually lifted up and emancipated through Christianity—a sweeping statement, which demands to be qualified! To begin with, the condition of women in antiquity was far from uniform and varied from country to country.[5] Furthermore, the idea of a continuous progress imputable as a whole to the rise and development of Christianity is a gratuitous assumption and at best a comforting, but often deceptive, generality. Finally, differences of activities or functions between men and women do not automatically determine a superior or inferior status.

My own task is presently to examine the biblical data in its historical context. What do the scriptures say, and how is what they say to be theologically interpreted? This article, therefore, is admittedly limited in scope. If I seem at times to venture "out of bounds," I shall do so at my own risk, leaving the formulation of final conclusions to my fellow theologians and ultimately to our hierarchs. All this being said, I am conscious of being unavoidably biased—for I am a man!

Feminine personal names offer valuable, though limited, hints as to the status of women in biblical culture and especially in relation to the religion and cult of Yahweh. The following list is given merely for the sake of illustration and does not claim to be exhaustive.[6] We shall use the spelling of the Revised Standard Version and give in parentheses an approximate transliteration of the original Hebrew, whenever this appears needed. The interpretation of these names is only tentative, inasmuch as their components have frequently been modified or as some incertitude remains on the roots or forms of verbs entering into their composition.

[5]One or two examples may suffice: the condition of women as reflected in the Middle Assyrian laws of the eleventh century B.C. is by far inferior to that of Babylonian women in the time of Hammurabi (eighteenth century B.C.); and until the recent feminist revolution, the freedom of Moslem women in cities was more restricted than that of Bedouin women, who retained a considerable initiative within the circle of their tasks in tent-life.

[6]For a complete survey, see Max Löhr, *Die Stellung des Weibes zu Jahve-Religion und Kult,* Beiträge zur Wissenschaft vom Alten Testament, 4 (Leipzig 1908).

44   WOMEN AND THE PRIESTHOOD

(1) *Theophoric names built with the element "Yahweh"
or the abridged form "Yah."* Abijah ('Abiyah, 2 Ch 29:1),
mother of Hezekiah, "Yahweh is my father"; the parallel
passage (2 Kg 18:2) gives the diminutive Abi ('Abî). Jeco-
liah (Yekolyâhu, 2 Kg 15:2), mother of Azariah, "Yahweh
is capable." Athaliah ('Athalyah, 2 Kg 11:1), mother of
Ahaziah, of uncertain meaning. Zeruiah (Tserûyah, 1 Ch
2:16), sister of David, also of uncertain meaning. Noadiah
(Nô'adyah, Ne 6:14), a prophetess, according to the Hebrew;
however, the LXX and Vulg. read in the masculine: τῷ
Νοαδίᾳ τῷ προφήτῃ, *Noadiae prophetae;* cf Ezra 8:33:
"Nô'adyah son of Binnuî, a Levite." To these names we
should probably add that of Shimrith (2 Ch 24:26), mother
of a murderer of Joash. Her name is the feminine form of
Shimri (1 Ch 4:37), which is probably an abbreviation of
Shemaryah, "Yahweh has kept."

(2) *Names built with "Yehô" (Yahu) or "Yô" (Yau).*
Jehoaddin (Yehô'addin, 2 Kg 14:2), mother of Amaziah,
"Yahweh gave joy." Jochebed (Yôkébéd, Ex 6:20), mother
of Aaron and Moses, "Yahweh is mighty."

(3) *Names built with "El."* As far as we are aware, the
only example of a feminine name in this category is Elisheba
('Elisheba', Ελισάβεθ, Ex 6:23), wife of Aaron, "My God
has sworn."

(4) *Names in which a term indicating a degree of kinship
is substituted for a divine name.* Abigail (1 Sm 25:3), wife
of Nabal and later of David, "My father [or, the father]
has given joy," and the variant Abigal (2 Sm 17:25), sister
of Zeruiah and mother of Joab. Abihail (1 Ch 2:29), wife
of a Yerahme'eli, also a niece of David (2 Ch 11:18), "My
father [or, the father] is valiant." Ahinoam (Ahinô'am, 1
Sm 14:50), wife of Saul, also a wife of David (2 Sm 2:2),
"My brother [or, the brother] is gracious."[7]

The names included in the first two categories above raise
the problem of the relation between the various forms of the
divine names. More precisely, the question is whether Yahweh

---

[7] Cf the Hebrew *nô'am,* "loveliness," "grace," from the verbal root *n-'-m;*
and the personal name *Na'aman* or *No'aman,* an epithet of Adonis-Tammuz.

(Y-h-w-h) is properly a name revealed to Moses from within the burning bush—as the J document and the priestly relation would have it—or whether it is meant as an identification of the mysterious Being with the God of Abraham, whatever the exact form of his name may have been—as the Elohist seems to assume. In the latter case, the revelation to Moses would not be the revelation of a new name, but rather the interpretation of a divine name already known to the patriarchs.

What presently interests us is that most Yahweh or Yehô theophoric names of men and women appear in the literature relative to the history of the kingdoms. This may be a reaction against Ba'alist influences—personal names formed with Ba'al having been artificially expurgated or derogatively interpreted by the Temple scribes. The Phoenician god *B'l z-b-l,* "Ba'al of the land," may very well hide under the name of Jezebel ('Izebel), the hated daughter of Ethba'al of Sidon (1 Kg 16:31), while the Hebrew scribe indulged in a scatological play of words on *zébél* (in Arabic, dung, refuse), by alluding to the obscene spectacle of the corpse of the queen torn by the dogs, her remains scattered "like dung [Hebr., *dômén*] in the fields of Jezréel" (2 Kg 9:37).

More important still is the fact that a number of Hebrew women shared with their husbands the honor of being named for the divinity. This invites us to discount the theory according to which biblical Yahwism was essentially a religion for men only. However, mere statistics of names give no indication of what part the women took in the cult, if they took any, and it remains, as we shall presently observe, that the ritual of the Hebrew sanctuaries regarded the priestly functions as a prerogative of men.

Biological factors had a large part in determining the social and religious condition of women and the role they played in the Old Testament community. We are reminded of them in the very first chapter of the Torah: the first human beings were created male and female (Gn 1:27). This, of course, is not a live record of facts. What the account of the six days of creation reflects is rather the thought and the faith of the Hebrews, constituted as a nation under the protection of Yahweh, with the date of the ninth century B.C. being generally accepted by modern critics for the earliest source of the Pentateuch. Under the biblical imagery, one fact is clear: the polarization of the sexes, which will impose itself all along the development of the species and which cannot be ignored or tampered with, short of unnatural and often disastrous consequences. By biblical charter, the woman is normally thought of as the companion of man and the mother of his children. Accordingly, the function of the woman as mother shall take exclusive precedence over any secondary avocation or individual circumstances. The motives or the incidence of apparent exceptions shall in no way invalidate the primacy of motherhood. "Adam called his wife's name Eve [Hebr., *Hawwah*, Ζωή] because she was the mother of all living" (radical *h-y-h*, but in Aramaic *h-w-h*; Gn 3:20). And when she gave birth to a son—the first man to be born of a woman—she called him Cain *(Qaîn)*, for she said: "I have gotten a man [*qânîthî*] through the power of Yahweh" (Gn 4:1).[8]

Feminine activities in Hebrew culture had their normal center in tent life and in the village house. Polygamy brought about a number of modalities in the constitution of the Hebrew family that would affect the role of women, inasmuch as the mother was the natural protector of the children of her womb (so-called "uterine groups" within the patriarchal family). Her first-born son felt responsible for his cadet brothers and sisters; similarly, the maternal uncle, *'am*, had a great influence in the relations between allied families. The social importance of the woman for the constitution of the tribe[9] was recognized in the authentic determination of a point of law by Moses himself, in the case of the succession of Zelophehad, of the clan of Machir in East Manasseh, who had died without sons. His daughters were habilitated to inherit the estate of the father, which would pass on to their prospective descendants, lest a house would be closed in Israel (Nb 27:1, 36:11).

Urban civilization, with its complex way of life under the

---

[8]Hebr., *'éth* Y-h-w-h, literally "with Yahweh"; LXX, διὰ τοῦ Θεοῦ; Vulg., *per dominum.*

[9]Short of any hazardous hypotheses on a primitive matriarchy.

Hebrew monarchy, obscured and often disturbed the simple pattern based on the primary role of the woman as mother, a biological "fix" (which could be controlled to some extent, but not essentially altered). Home arts and crafts, which together with the care of children filled the life of women, came to be practiced commercially in the bazaar, and the free ways of the camp or of the village were gradually replaced by a more polished code of behavior—not necessarily more ethical, but still a far cry from the Moslem or Hindu *purdah*. The evolution of American life within the space of a few generations offers a striking illustration: from immigrant settlers and colonists, the frontier, the homestead, to the megalopolis and the suburbanite clusters.

A certain emancipation of city women was bound to take place in Israel, hastened by the circumstances of the postexilic resettlement and the invasion of Hellenism. We need not, however, regard the encomium of the ideal house mother (Pr 31:10-31) as a realistic picture—it is rather an exercise in style by a scribe not a little proud of his literary skill. In the New Testament, we catch a glimpse of a career woman: Lydia, St. Paul's hostess at Philippi. We would like to know more about her. A Gentile from the Hellenized city of Thyatira in Asia Minor, where she may have been in contact with the Jewish community, she carried on in continental Greece what seems to have been a prosperous business in Tyrian purple (Ac 16:14).

By and large, however, the biblical writings, both Old and New Testament, offer to us the picture of a man's world.[10] Public life is a masculine prerogative and burden: "Man goes forth unto his work and unto his service till evening" (Ps 104:23), in peace, and especially in time of war. We do not see any Amazons, unless we count as war heroines such exceptional characters as Jael, wife of Heber the Qenite, who murdered the defeated Sisera as he sought to take shelter in her tent (Jg 4:17-21); or the woman of Thebez who cast a

---

[10]Women rulers were not uncommon in Hellenistic times, especially in Egypt, where the example of Hatshepsuth (eighteenth dynasty) could be regarded as a precedent. However, statues of the queen represent her as sporting the postiche Osirian goatee.

millstone on the head of Abimelek and cracked his skull while he made ready to storm the rampart (Jg 9:52-54); or "the wise woman" who tossed the head of the rebel Sheba ben Bichri over the wall of Abel Beth Ma'achah during the siege of that city by Joab (2 Sm 20:16-22).[11] As for Judith, "the Jewess," she belongs in what seems to have been a patriotic "short story" rather than a historical narrative.

Thus far, scriptural evidence does not support the thesis of a radical inferiority of women in biblical culture. They have their own sphere of activity different from that of men, and except for a few activities common to both sexes, these spheres are not interchangeable. But the personalities and specific activities of a man and his wife (or wives) are not to be adjudged as of unequal worth. Eve was created as Adam's partner, his "opposite number," *kenêgdô* (Gn 2:18), as bone of his bone and flesh of his flesh (Gn 2:23). But the delicate balance was compromised by the sin of the first human couple, to which outbursts of wild passion and the eventual tyranny of husbands is traced (Gn 3:16). The usual interpretation of the Hebrew correlatives *ba'al* and *be'ûlah*, "lord over the wife" and "under marital lordship," is generally overdone; the etymological alliteration is untranslatable in correct English and would be something more like "husband" and "husband-ed." This does not mean much more than the ancient Roman formula: "Where you will be Caius, I shall be Caia." What is basic is the complementarity of the sexes. Husband and wife are in partnership with regard to family life and eventually for occupations in or outside the home. I am thinking here of Aquila and Priscilla, the devoted hosts of St. Paul in Corinth (Ac 18:2).

The scriptures record several instances of women endowed with charismatic power, the exercise of which follows no established pattern, depending solely on the Spirit which moves them "where it listeth" in circumstances ultimately determined or controlled by God. The gift of prophecy is not uncommon. The prophet—*nâbî* (fem., *nebî'ah*), προφή-της (fem., προφῆτις), *propheta* (fem., *prophetis, prophe-*

---

[11]In the latter two episodes, the fate of the victims is aggravated by the irony of being slain by women.

tissa)—is essentially a person called by God to proclaim his message to men. Through the prophet, God makes known his secrets, warns of punishment, encourages through exhortations and promises of grace, and occasionally discloses what is going to pass in the future. We seem to have retained only the latter aspect and neglected or forgotten the religious and ethical substance or the requirements of prophecy. The message was often recorded in rhythmic prose, either by the prophet himself or by some of his disciples. A study of the form and technique of a given message may help us to decide on that either/or, but it would be most imprudent to deduce from this a radical distinction between old-fashioned prophets, those who do not write, and the prophet-writers like Isaiah or Jeremiah and Jeremiah's secretary Baruch. Obviously, the words prophecy, prophet and prophetess are not to be understood univocally, but with some elasticity, as suggested by the context and the contents of the message. As a matter of fact, the Bible does not distinguish sharply between prophetic and poetic inspiration. Poetry is also a gift of God, who speaks through the poet; the poet is not a mere maker of rhymes or aligner of meters, a cheap versifier. A genuine gift of true poetry has been observed frequently among uncultured Italian, Romanian or Greek peasant women, seized by the emotion of a funeral wake.

The Bible did not fail to record the paean of victory after the miraculous crossing of the Sea of Reeds, when "Miriam the prophetess took her timbrel in her hand, and all the women went out after her with timbrels and with dances, and Miriam intoned: 'Sing ye to the Lord, for he has triumphed gloriously; the horse and the rider has he thrown into the sea' " (Ex 15:20-21). Miriam's words are the refrain of the canticle credited by the Yahwist to Moses (Ex 15:1-18)[12]— the theme of our first ode at Matins. In the critical days of the settlement in Canaan, when the immigrants had to face the reaction of the indigenous populations they had overrun, there arose a "woman prophet" (*'ishah nebî'ah,* γυνὴ προφῆτις), who led the choirs of the Israelites after their

[12]Miriam is the sister of Moses and Aaron (Nb 26:59); Moses is the prototype of all prophets (Dt 18:15; Ho 12:13).

victory by the river Qishôn (Jg 5:1-31): "When in Israel they untie their hair [i.e., set out to holy war], when the people willingly rise,[13] bless ye the Lord! Hear, O kings, give ear, O princes, I, even I, to Yahweh will I sing!" Deborah's war song extols Jael the Qenite and stigmatizes those who had not joined in the common struggle for independence in the name of Yahweh. For the charismatic office of Deborah is not merely that of a prophetess and choir leader. The book of Judges (4:4-5) describes by way of introduction how "she judged the people in those days, as she sat under the palmtree which was named for her between Ramah and Bethel in the highlands of Ephraim, and the Benê Israel came up to her for all judgment." Her horizon is not limited by the clannish outlook of villagers snug in their valleys; it extends to all the tribes. Her function is that of a *shôphét*, a Hebrew name for the charismatic chieftain who sits in counsel, hears the causes of God's people and leads the tribes in time of stress. These *shôphetim* of the book of Judges must be distinguished from the *shôphetim* of Carthage, who were regular office holders of what we might call the "establishment."

In the eighth century B.C., Isaiah referred to his wife as "the prophetess," who bore him several children called by symbolic names (Is 8:3-4). This does not necessarily mean that she had prophesied in her own right; it is generally agreed that in this instance, prophetess means simply the wife of the prophet, as we refer familiarly to the wife of a Greek priest as the πρεσβυτέρα. But women prophets did continue in the period of the kingdoms. During the reign of Josiah, king of Judah, a prophetess, Huldah, consulted by a delegation of priests and officers of the kingdom, authenticated the book of the Torah recently discovered in the Temple,[14] confirmed in Yahweh's name the verdict against an unfaithful nation and predicted that the king would be "gathered to his fathers" before the punishment would take place (2 Kg 22: 14-20; 2 Ch 34:22-28).

---

[13]From the Hebrew; cf Vulg., *qui sponte obtulistis de Israel animas vestras ad periculum.* A different reading is in the LXX: ἀπεκαλύφθη ἀποκά-λυμμα.

[14]Believed to be the original nucleus of the book of Deuteronomy.

The age of the Old Testament prophecy came to an end with the announcement by Joel (2:28-32; cf Ac 2:17-21) that, in the days of the Messiah, "your sons and daughters shall prophesy," for Yahweh will "pour out his spirit over all flesh"—a prophecy realized literally in the days of the early Christian Church, when St. Paul listed among the gifts of the Holy Spirit the charism of prophecy, bestowed on men and women alike (1 Co 12:28), and of which the four virgin daughters of Philip the Evangelist were favored (Ac 21:9). But there were also false prophets and prophetesses. Some of them could better be described as inspired by a spirit of deceit (1 Kg 22:20-23), whereas many were downright fakes, like those bitterly denounced by Jeremiah. The witch of Endor is a notorious example of the former category (1 Sm 28:7 ff), whereas Noadiah, the prophetess[15] who opposed the restoration of the walls of Jerusalem under Nehemiah, belongs to the latter (Ne 6:14).

Biological factors play no part in the exercise of the prophetic charism *qua* charism, because it draws its origin not from the will of men but from the Holy Spirit. As we have tried to show above, the role of female prophets in the religious history of Israel has been prestigious. The lesser incidence of prophetic manifestations through women, compared with the greater number of male prophets, is immaterial, depending as it does on divine economy and on the fact that scriptural records were the work of male scribes of the palace or of the Temple.

On the other hand, the difference of sexes was a determining element in the organization of Hebrew worship through human agencies: patriarchal customs, and rules codified by Moses. To recall at this point the pieces of advice he received from his father-in-law (Ex 18:13-27) may not be totally irrelevant, although the attempt to trace back the Mosaic institution wholesale to Midianite or Qenite origins remains an overdone hypothesis too farfetched for plausibility. The biological conditioning of the cultic requirements of

---

[15]According to the Hebrew and the Vulgate. But the LXX, as noted above, reads a masculine; the theophoric name suits a man or a woman equally well.

Yahwism is nowhere more clearly manifested than in the
laws on the clean and the unclean, respectively *tâhôr* and
tâmè' (Lv 15). The final enactment of that casuistry is indeed
late; modern criticism dates Leviticus to the postexilic period,
in possible connection with the reorganization of the cult
under Ezra and Nehemiah. But it harks back to precepts edited
by Moses and Aaron, and these again must be evaluated
against a background of common Semitic practices, rites and
religious taboos to which they are related in form and spirit,
or against which they react. There is an evident relationship
between ritual purity and bodily cleanliness, but this relationship is left undefined, even though ritual transgressions and
offenses against persons or against the community call for
different kinds of expiatory sacrifices.[16]

Crucial in this complex development is the ancient idea
that the soul of man is in the blood, as the fluid of life, and
life belongs exclusively to God (Lv 17:10-14). Hence, anyone who sheds blood in violation of Yahweh's precepts,
except in the specific instances spelled out in the Torah, is
barred from participation in the religious life of the community until adequate satisfaction is offered for the removal
of the impurity thus contracted. Similarly, everything that is
related from near or far to generation, i.e., infusion of life,
is bound to affect the state of ritual purity of men and, more
so, of women. Their menstruations make them periodically
impure (we might say, taboo), as do the processes of child-
birth, or any pathological condition resulting in hemorrhages
and the like. The law prescribes a detailed ritual for readmit-
ting a woman after the impurity contracted in childbirth (Lv
12) — a ritual to which the Theotokos herself submitted,
"when the days of their purification were fulfilled" (Lk 2:22
ff).[17]

Biological factors determine clearly the status of the
Israelite woman in relation to the Aaronic priesthood. The
fact that some of them are chosen to be the wives of priests

[16]See R. de Vaux, *Ancient Israel* 2 (New York: McGraw-Hill, 1961)
429f.
[17]Note the reading: "for *their* purification." The infant Jesus had to be
redeemed, according to the law of the first-born. The churching of women
is the Christian adaptation of the Old Testament rite.

does not confer on them any privilege, but rather obligations. A priest's daughter who sins publicly must be put to death by fire (Lv 21:9), and a priest's daughter who has married a stranger will be readmitted to the family table only after she has become a widow or has been repudiated by her husband; then she will be permitted to partake of the portions allotted to the priests for their meals (Lv 22:12-13).

As a rule, women were, so to speak, kept on the outskirts of the sanctuary. The book of Exodus relates how they contributed gifts of jewelry and in weaving and embroidering the veils and curtains of the tabernacle and the vestments of the priests (Ex 35:20-29). However, the custody of the sacred ornaments, vessels and utensils had been reserved to the sons of Kohath (Nb 4:4). No feminine names appear in the Chronicler's lists of Levites in charge of the musical service and choirs of the Temple, with the possible exception of the three daughters of Heman, who sang under his direction together with their fourteen brothers (1 Ch 25:5-6).[18]

Obscure mentions are made of women on guard duty at the entrance of the so-called "tent of meeting" (Ex 33:7) and at the gate of the sanctuary of Shiloh (1 Sm 2:22). The latter passage relates the misconduct of the sons of Eli, who abused some of these women. It is possible, though improbable, that we have here an allusion to a regular case of "ritual prostitution," discretely amended by the scribes. At any rate, the exclusion of Israelite women from the sacred precincts of the Temple became stricter as a reflex of defense against Ba'alist contaminations during the entire period of the kingdoms. The books of Kings and the Chronicles refer to the valiant but not very successful efforts of some reformers to eliminate once and for all the prostitutes of the Ba'alist cults, "under every green tree" and even in the halls of the Temple.

The postexilic speculations on ritual purity are best illustrated in Ezekiel's vision of the ideal Temple of Yahweh, which was to be architecturally transposed into Herod's

---

[18]The Annals of Sennacherib, describing the campaign against Hezekiah, mentions the tribute sent by the king to Nineveh, which included, among other valuables, concubines and male and female singers. See J. Pritchard, *Ancient Near Eastern Texts* (Princeton: Princeton University Press, 1950) 288.

Temple, where a series of courtyards "filtered" the worshipers according to the degree of their consecration to Yahweh. Women were assigned the eastern courtyard, which they shared with male Israelites temporarily or permanently impure. They were not allowed to proceed to the inner courtyard, or "Courtyard of Israel." In late Judaism, women had in synagogues their reserved section, usually some tribune or upper gallery, according to an exegesis of the Talmud of Babylon (Sukkoth V, 1:55b).

The epistle to the Hebrews is the locus for the theme of Christ as the priest of the eternal covenant. It provided western medieval theology with prooftexts for the doctrine of the "priestly office" of Christ, and the Eastern Church with the epistle readings for the liturgy of the Entrance of the Theotokos into the Temple—the Hypapante, when the infant Jesus was met by Simeon and Anna[19]—and the third, fourth and fifth Sundays in Lent, preparatory to the Passion and to Pascha. Thus, we should be prompted to reflect on how the title of priest came to be attributed to Christ. It is not because he was compared to the human priest, but quite the reverse: the eternal priesthood of Christ is the root of the analogy implicitly recognized by our liturgists and elaborated by the scholastic theologians.

As a matter of fact, the office of Christ in the general economy of salvation is always contrasted with the service of Aaronic priests in the Temple. It is eternal, *versus* temporary; universal, *versus* national. The Aaronic high priest entered once a year into the "Holy of Holies"; our high priest entered once and for all into the sanctuary of heaven, with his lifegiving blood, not with the blood of victims, and having trampled down death by death, he rose from the grave as a conqueror. An Aaronic priest served in the Temple at the turn of his class; but the obedience of our high priest encompassed the entire course of his human existence. In order to describe it, we may borrow the words of our liturgical anam-

[19]The Feast of the Entrance is better known in the West as the Presentation of the Virgin Mary, and the Hypapante as the Purification of the Virgin, also called Candlemas (*la Chandeleur*), when beeswax candles are offered at mass for the service of the altar.

nesis, "remembering all those things which have come to pass for us: the Cross, the Tomb, the Resurrection on the third day, the Ascension into heaven, the sitting at the right hand, and the second and glorious coming."

To sum up, the Aaronic priesthood was but the imperfect foreshadowing of the service of Christ, whose resurrection would consummate and manifest the reality of his priesthood. For the author of Hebrews, the comparison between Aaron and Jesus Christ ends in an irreducible opposition, and the authentic type of the one eternal priest is to be found in the mysterious figure of Melchizedek. He is mentioned first in the fourteenth chapter of Genesis, which narrates how he met Abraham returning victorious from his battle against the four kings. King of Salem[20] and priest of *'El-'Elyôn,* the Most High—one of the names given to him whom no name can describe—the personality of the king-priest is as much of a riddle as his origins: "without father, without mother, without genealogy, having neither beginning of days, nor end of life," writes the author of Hebrews (7:3). In other words, he appeared on the stage of history, but he is not of history, and he transcends the limitations of the human predicament. His role is prophetic through and through. David saw in him the type of the Messiah, "priest forever according to the order of Melchizedek" (Ps 110:4). Thus, the author of Hebrews and the entire tradition after him hail Jesus Christ with the words of the Psalm.

Nobody would deny that the Theotokos was associated in the process of our salvation in some way, but which way? The rhetorical argument of some fathers, namely, that since Christ is the new Adam, then Mary must be the new Eve, is not sufficient. Neither scripture nor tradition, not even the hyperbolic acclamations of the Akathistos hymn, attribute to her any participation in the eternal priesthood of Christ. If a few well-meaning but ill-advised opinions seem to open such a prospect, they belong rather in baroque or romantic literature and have little or no doctrinal foundation.

[20]Salem was identified in Jewish tradition with Jerusalem, and this identification has generally been accepted by the fathers. It has no essential bearing on the theological significance of the narrative.

The dignity of Mary was in the consent she gave to the angel of the annunciation to being the maidservant of the Lord, and she was that maidservant to her last breath—the mother of the eternally begotten, who had need of her to be born a man, to be fed and anxiously brought up by her during his childhood. She wondered about him, could not understand the mystery hidden in her son—who does? At Cana of Galilee, she made no miracle, but uttered a prayer. When Christ offered himself in the unique sacrifice of which he was both the priest and the victim, Mary stood by the cross, recapitulating in herself the suffering of all the tragic figures of Old Testament women: Hagar in the desert, where she was driven with Ishmael through the jealousy of Sarah (Gn 21:14-16); the voice that was "heard in Ramah, wailing and loud lamentation, Rachel weeping for her children, and she would not be comforted, because they are no more" (Jr 31: 15); Rizpah keeping watch over the bodies of her sons and chasing away the birds and beasts of prey (2 Sm 21:10). One of the last words of Jesus was for entrusting Mary to John, the chosen disciple, unto whom she would be a mother (Jn 19:26-27).

The Latin Church, on the Friday before Holy Week, commemorates the "Compassion" of the Virgin, and the station is in the church of "St. Mary of the Martyrs."[21] We are reminded in the office of the day that all the pains Christ endured in his agony, she bore in her heart,[22] and she could rightly appropriate the words of the first Lamentation (1:12): "All ye who pass by, behold and see if there is any sorrow like unto my sorrow."[23] More than any other human being, Mary suffered with her son, yet it is in no way suggested that in this she made an act of a priest. The Creed goes on: "And He rose from the dead and ascended into heaven," his sacrifice being presented to the Father on "the altar on high, before the face of the Divine Majesty."[24] The Orthodox Church has

---

[21]During Advent and Lent and for certain feasts, the liturgical service in the diocese of Rome is performed in a different church every day, with the Pope or some high dignitary officiating.

[22]The reference is to an antiphon of the first Vespers.

[23]Lesson 1 at Matins.

[24]Eucharistic Canon of the Roman Mass.

always been extremely reserved in interpreting the association of Mary to these glorious mysteries. It does not wish to speculate on her bodily assumption into heaven, which remains a pious belief not, however, unanimously or unambiguously backed by tradition.[25] It prefers to speak of the "sleeping in" of the Virgin, whose soul, under the appearance of a diminutive feminine figure, is represented in some icons as arising from the body which lies on the bier. We might recall here the mention that is made after the eucharistic epiclesis of "our most holy, immaculate, most blessed and glorious Lady Theotokos and ever-virgin Mary," the first to be remembered among "those who have gone to their rest," and *for whom* we offer the rational worship, of which Christ is the priest.

The New Testament writings leave us dramatically short of information on the organization of the Church during the decades immediately following the resurrection. The Acts of the Apostles refers to a communal worship of the brethren, who prayed in the Temple at the appointed hours and assembled in private houses (Ac 2:46). The house of Mary, the mother of John Mark, was a preferred place of meeting (Ac 12:12). It was to become the "Holy Zion, mother of all churches." But we know precious little of the regime of the assemblies, who would lead in prayer and who would preside "at the breaking of the bread," prior to the institutionalization of the Church. We can but use the clues scattered in the descriptions of the Christian communities visited by St. Paul in Asia Minor and in Greece, and compare them with what we know of the organization of the synagogues in the Jewish diaspora, since most of the earliest churches developed in a Jewish setting.

This would partially explain why the officers of such churches were invariably men, and how one of them was chosen to preside over the assembly for the daily prayers and at the eucharistic meal. The apostles, singly or in a group, were influential in approval or confirmation of such choices

[25]The bodily assumption of Mary was defined in 1950 by Pope Pius XII. The arguments in support of the definition are based on the previous definition of the Immaculate Conception, which involves contestable theories on original sin.

and in the advice or admonitions they could give to communities visited, but it is coincidental that some of their
number, like James and (later) Peter, became heads of local
churches. Apparently St. Paul never was.

The late epistles, especially the first to Timothy and the
letter to Titus, go one step further and witness to the rise
of a clergy in a more advanced phase of the apostolic age,
among Christian communities increasingly open to the Gentiles, and in which ethnic differences were gradually obliter-
ated. The Church was on its way toward a hierarchic organization: the bishop, surrounded by his presbyters and a corps
of deacons who served at first at menial tasks—cf the institution of the "seven" (Ac 6:1-6)—but were later aggregated
to the clergy and entrusted with liturgical functions.[26]

It was felt, on doctrinal grounds, that the central place
of the eucharist in the life of the Church and its direct connection with the self-oblation of Christ on the cross and his
resurrection demanded that the consecration of the bread and
the wine be reserved to those constituted in priestly office and
made partakers of the priesthood of Christ. Other parts of
their ministry could eventually be shared with subaltern
clergy, laymen or women, but eucharistic functions belonged
exclusively to the bishop and the presbyteral college. The
Theotokos had not been called to offer the sacrifice on Cal-
vary; neither would women be admitted as members of the
Church's sacred priesthood. Early Christianity knew nothing
of women priests. This does not mean that women were
regarded as second-class members of the Church. It must be
admitted that personally St. Paul never gave women more
than what he esteemed was their due, and in this he was
certainly not lavish. He reacted sour against untimely charismatic manifestations, but his chief concern was to keep order
in the assemblies of the Church and restore among the faithful a sense of relative values by ousting quacks and preventing
a display of untested spirits (1 Co 11:2-16, 14:34).

Two categories of women may be singled out which came
to be recognized very early in the Church, with a marked

[26]It is not within the scope of this paper to discuss the nature of the
presbyteral institution in relation to the episcopate.

tendency to institutionalization. The first is that of the deaconesses, whose functions were at first casual, but who later were inducted into the standing personnel of the churches. There was obviously a place and a role for women in the daily life of the local community: visiting and helping women fallen in sickness and indigence, "alone in the world," assisting in the baptismal immersion of women, and the like. St. Paul, writing to the Romans, recommended Phoebe, who was "a deaconess of the church which is at Cenchreae, a helper of many, and of myself as well" (Rm 16:1-2).[27] The second category is that of the widows, who were particularly qualified for those labors of love, on account of the discretion one would expect of mature women (1 Tm 5:3 ff).[28]

That these offices, entrusted to women with reservations we may deem excessive, can and should be expanded as boldly as shall prove expedient, nobody would deny. But the priesthood, in the sense of the sacramental, eucharistic priesthood, is by no means synonymous with that common ministry in which we all share,[29] as we are "built up into a spiritual house, to be a holy priesthood to offer spiritual sacrifices acceptable to God through Jesus Christ" (1 Pt 2:5).

All the observations we have made by scanning the Old and the New Testaments, cumulatively taken, are enough to authorize a prejudgment against the accession of women to the hierarchic priesthood. Presumption, however, is not conviction. A mere survey of biblical evidence is not sufficient for solving the problem conclusively, for the scriptures are not to be read independently of tradition, the παράδοσις, which is the organ of divine revelation, and lives in the traditions of the Church. Tradition is necessarily influenced by historical and cultural contingencies; if it were not so, our teaching

[27]The periphrase οὖσαν διάκονον may indicate a hesitation on the part of the writer. The noun, in spite of its masculine ending, is used for both genders; it does not necessarily designate a specific title. The Vulgate reads: *quae est in ministerio ecclesiae quae est in Cenchris.*

[28]Information on the status of these persons can be found in commentaries on the Pauline epistles, especially in C. Spicq, *Les épîtres pastorales* (Paris 1969) XLVII-XLVIII of the Introduction.

[29]A deacon may be listed as "clergy" and receive communion at the altar, but it is significant that, when he dies, the office of burial is that of laymen.

would be a gratuitous ideology resting on shaky foundations. It is true that cultures have a life of their own: history records their birth, their growing to maturity, their eventual obsolescence and their extinction. Yet they are an integral part in the very texture of church tradition and must not be forgotten or brushed aside. The life of the Church may call for new forms, but these shall have no chance if they are not traditionally rooted. This is why, if I am asked bluntly whether, in my opinion, women should be ordained to the priesthood, I will, even if I seem to overstep the limits of this essay, give an equally blunt answer: no!

Presbytides or Female Presidents

Canon 11, Council of Laodicea

By Nicholas Afanasiev*

"There shall be no appointment of so-called presbytides or female presidents in the Church." This puzzling canon is no less enigmatic than the Council of Laodicea itself, about which we know neither the exact date nor membership. In a short preface to the canons it is stated: "The Holy Synod of various provinces of Asia, assembled at Laodicea in Phrygia, established the following canons." This note does little more than restate the council's name, since not even the specific provinces represented are mentioned. We are equally uncertain about the council's date. Usually it is assumed that it took place in the second half of the fourth century, after the Council of Nicea. These unknowns do not exhaust our difficulties. There is no complete text of the Laodicean canons. We must rely on a type of synopsis, as the canons have come down to us in abbreviated form.[1] Although there is no reason to suppose that the abbreviation was rendered carelessly or unskilfully, a

*Nicholas Afanasiev was Professor of Canon Law at the St. Sergius Theological Institute in Paris from 1930 until his death in 1966. Born in Odessa in 1893, he served for many years as a priest in the Russian Orthodox Church and authored numerous books and articles, mainly on ecclesiological issues. His major work, in addition to *The Table of the Lord* and *The Ministry of Lay People in the Church,* was his doctoral dissertation, *The Church of the Holy Spirit.* The present article was originally published in Russian in *Vestnik RKhD,* no. 2 (1957) 13-24, and was translated into English by John Jillions.

[1]For the text, see Mansi, *Sacrorum conciliorum* 2:564-74; and the critical text in J.B. Pitra, *Juris ecclesiastici graecorum historia et monumenta* 1 (Rome 1862) 495-504.

complete text would no doubt make canon 11 less enigmatic.

What is this canon referring to? Who were these presbytides or female presidents? Historians and canonists have yet to agree on answers to these questions. This is not at all surprising, since we have no direct information about presbytides or female presidents from sources other than canon 11. All that can be clearly stated is that this canon refers to persons appointed by the local churches to fulfil a specific ministry. In his commentary on this canon, the twelfth-century canonist Zonaras writes: "The ancients had a number of customs that either changed over the course of time, fell out of use or came to be forbidden by canons. One such custom was the appointing of several elderly women in the church to be presbytides and calling them 'presidents.' They watched over the women who came to church, and like teachers instructed them in church order, showing them where and how they ought to stand. Thus, the canon prescribes that these positions should not exist, nor should women be called such."[2] Balsamon almost repeats Zonaras: "In ancient times certain venerable women, who held the position of presbytis in the cathedral churches, took care that the other women kept good and modest order. But from their habit of abusing this good office, either through their arrogance or through base self-seeking, scandal arose. Therefore the fathers prohibited the existence of any more such women called presbytides or presidents."[3]

These commentaries add nothing to our understanding of the canon, since it is apparent that besides the text of the canon neither Zonaras nor Balsamon had any further information about presbytides. It is noteworthy that neither of these writers mentioned deaconesses. It follows that they did not equate presbytides with deaconesses. They evidently knew that the institution of deaconesses had not been forbidden in the fourth century or even in their own era, although by that time the office of deaconess had become simply a position of honor, and not an active ministry. For this reason we must reject the frequently heard supposition that presbytides were

[2]Commentary on canon 11 of Laodicea.
[3]Commentary on the same canon.

deaconesses, or at least the eldest of the deaconesses. No facts exist to support this supposition. Just as unlikely is the hypothesis that presbytides were "archdeaconesses" who supposedly presided over the deaconesses.[4] Besides being unlikely, this hypothesis does not help clarify the problem, since it simply replaces one obscure term with another.

Judging from what we already know about the ministry of women in the early Church, we can postulate still another hypothesis. Was it not church widows that the Laodicean council had in mind in its eleventh canon, referring to presbytides or presidents? To support this idea we can cite a comment by Epiphanius. He noted that the eldest among the widows were called presbytides. He wrote about this in reference to the heresy of the Collyridians, affirming, however, that the Church had never appointed presbyteresses or priestesses.[5] We have no reason to doubt Epiphanius' information, regardless of the polemical character of his comments. Therefore, on the basis of his testimony, we can say that presbytides existed in some churches at the very least.

This conclusion is in part supported by the *Testament of our Lord Jesus Christ,* a Syrian document of the fifth century. In addition to widows and deaconesses, the composer of this document mentions presbytides (if we follow the Latin translation of this work), but nowhere does he speak of their functions or how they are appointed. Also, what is more astonishing, he does not mention presbytides in describing the arrangement of participants during the church assembly or in the order of communion.[6]

The most likely explanation for this omission, assuming that the mention of presbytides in the *Testament* is not an interpolation, is that presbytides were the eldest of the widows and therefore were included under the rank or number of widows. In other words, the term "presbytis," as it is used both in the *Testament* and by Epiphanius, did not denote a

[4]See V.V. Bolotov, *Lektsii po istorii drevnei tserkvi,* 3d ed. (St. Petersburg 1900) 157; Hefele-Leclercq, *Histoire des Conciles* 1 (Paris 1907) 1003-4.

[5]*Panarion* 79:4.

[6]I.E. Rahmani, ed., *Testamentum Domini Nostri Jesu Christi* (Mainz 1899) 37, 47.

specific function but was a term of honor ascribed to some of the widows. The term "female president," meanwhile, is not found in either of these sources. If this term had existed in the Syrian Church, then the compiler of the *Testament* would certainly have used it, given his tendency to promote widows ahead of deaconesses. Although the *Testament* states that widows supervised the deaconesses, it should not be concluded that widows were presidents. As we shall see, this term did not refer to someone who was the head of some group of church members, such as deaconesses, but denoted persons who held a special place in the church assembly. Although widows had a distinguished position in the church hierarchy, according to the *Testament,* they did not stand higher than deacons and did not occupy the first place in the church assembly. For this reason it is completely unlikely that the widows and presbytides of Epiphanius and the *Testament* can be equated with the presbytides and presidents of the Laodicean council.

Thus, we must conclude that the eleventh canon refers to some totally unique ministry that perhaps was similar to the ministry of widows but not identical to it. In order to define this ministry we must begin with the canon itself, or more exactly, with the terms that designate this ministry. The term πρεσβῦτις itself tells us almost nothing. In the letter to Titus 2:3-5, as in other canonical documents, it means an elderly woman.[7] It continues to have this meaning in later canonical documents. Accordingly, in the *Apostolic Constitutions* the terms "presbytis" and "presbytera" signify an elderly woman in general, or a widow at least sixty years of age and under the care of the local church.[8] In and of itself, this term, like its male counterpart "elder" (πρεσβύτης), does not indicate a specific ministry. As we have already seen in the *Testament of our Lord Jesus Christ* and in Epiphanius, "presbytis" refers to the oldest of the widows. The ministry of these honored widows was not defined by this term but by the ministry of widows themselves.

The key to the riddle of canon 11 of Laodicea must be

---

[7]C. Spicq, *Les épîtres pastorales* (Paris 1947) 250-1.
[8]*Apostolic Constitutions* 2:28, 57; 3:5.

sought in another term used therein: presbytides are also called "presidents." Apparently the term προκαθήμεναι (female presidents) is unique to this canon, but the masculine version (προκαθήμενοι) is not only common in early Christian writings, but has a well-defined, quite unambiguous liturgical meaning. From the very beginning the eucharistic assembly had a definite order for the arrangement of participants (see Jm 2:2-4; Rv 4:2-4). With the discontinuation of the special ministries of the apostolic age and the rise of the clergy this order was gradually modified, but it remained fundamentally the same. The *Apostolic Constitutions* paint the following picture of the eucharistic gathering: "In the center [i.e., in the center of the building] should be the bishop's throne with the presbyters sitting on either side of him; standing on either side should be the deacons, agile and simply dressed, for they can be compared to seamen who stand on either side of a ship and oversee the oarsmen; in accord with the deacons' instructions, the laity should sit in another part of the church keeping silence and good order, but the women separately and keeping silence."[9] The *Testament of our Lord Jesus Christ* gives an even more detailed picture of the arrangement: the bishop's place is in the center, with places for presbyters on either side; widows are on the left, behind the presbyters; deacons, readers and subdeacons stand in order on the right, behind the presbyters.[10]

The places in the eucharistic assembly were not designated haphazardly or according to the personal worthiness of the participants. One's place in the eucharistic assembly was connected to one's ministry; conversely, one who performed a particular ministry had his own specific place. "Presidents" were those who occupied the first place in the assembly. This place was an expression of their ministry: as those carrying out the ministry of leadership, they stood at the head of the local church. Since apostolic times the "presidents" had been presbyters, one of whom was the bishop. Since he held the central place among presbyters, he stood in front of the

[9] *Apostolic Constitutions* 2:57. See also Gregory Dix, *The Shape of the Liturgy* (London: Dacre Press, 1945) 24.
[10] *Testamentum*, 47.

whole church, as her head, during the celebration of the
eucharist—i.e., he was her presiding officer. And since place
expressed ministry, no one except the bishop and presbyters
could hold the first place, no matter what their own importance, including prophets and teachers. The *Shepherd of
Hermas* condemns those prophets who sought to have the
"first place" in the church assembly.[11] This indicates that
some prophets tried to usurp a place among the presbyters
on the strength of their prophetic ministry, or—even more
likely—they sought to be appointed presbyters. Hermas himself refused to occupy the first place, pointing out that it belongs to the presbyters, and only accepted it after the repeated
order of the "aged woman" in his vision.[12] For him, as for
other Roman Christians, there was no doubt that the first place
belonged to the presbyters.

There can be no other meaning for the feminine form of
"president." Female presidents could only have been those
who held the first place in the eucharistic assembly. If presbyters were presidents, then female presidents must have been
female presbyters, for only on the strength of that ministry
could they occupy the first place. We must immediately
qualify this by saying that these presidents did not necessarily
have liturgical duties. This is not the place to discuss the
much debated question of whether presbyters held the ministry of priesthood from the start; however, independent of this
question, it is a fact that the first presbyters had no liturgical
functions. They formed the "presbyterium," that is, the
council or, as St. Ignatius of Antioch expressed it, the
synedrion or "senate" of the church. This body administrated
the church jointly with the bishop. Presbyters were permitted
to celebrate the holy mysteries if the bishop specially charged
them to perform the eucharist. But this took place in exceptional circumstances, since the bishop himself celebrated the
eucharist as the natural expression of his leadership whenever
he was present at the assembly. In the second half of the
third century, presbyters who headed church assemblies at
secondary liturgical centers within the jurisdiction of the

[11]See mandate 11.
[12]See vision 3.

local church or, anachronistically, who headed "parishes," were given clearly defined liturgical functions. However, this does not mean that every presbyter who joined the presbyterium performed the sacraments. Those who did not have "parishes" continued simply in the performance of their previous ministry, i.e., the ministry of leadership which the whole presbyterium shared under the headship of the bishop. Therefore, if local churches—we are speaking of orthodox churches—had the kind of presbytides or female presidents that the Laodicean council describes, then it would be extremely unlikely that the bishop would have charged them to perform any sacraments. Christian consciousness, as in Judaism, firmly refused to recognize a priestly dignity in women. To be convinced of this it is enough to recall what Epiphanius wrote in reference to the Collyridian heresy. If they existed, "female presidents" could only have continued in that capacity before the middle of the third century, while the teaching about the presbyterial ministry was still developing.

Analyzing the terms of canon 11 of the Council of Laodicea, we are led to the following conclusion: presbytides or female presidents were female presbyters who apparently did not have defined liturgical functions. This situation could be compared to that of deaconesses, who were female deacons but had extremely limited, strictly ancillary liturgical functions. However, the riddle of the canon is not solved by this explanation. If female presidents existed—and it seems they did according to the Laodicean council—and if they were a Church-wide phenomenon, then we should have evidence about them in at least several other church documents. The absence of such documentation is what is so puzzling.

Possibly, we might cite as evidence Romans 16:1-2: "I commend to you our sister Phoebe, a deaconess of the church at Cenchreae, that you may receive her in the Lord as befits the saints and help her in whatever she may require from you, for she has been a helper [προστάτις] of many and of myself as well." Could Phoebe have been one of these female presidents of a church, as the term προστάτις might indicate? The masculine προστάτης had a variety of meanings: someone in front, and, by extension, one who stands in front

of a mobilized detachment of soldiers; later, it meant someone in a democratic government who was the head of a party.
This term also denoted a protector or defender, in particular
a protector or patron of foreigners in Athens. Finally, in the
religious sense προστάτης referred to a man who stood
before the altar. In a more limited sense, Flavius Josephus
used the term in reference to the emperor. In Egypt it was
associated with the head of a religious society.[13]

That the apostle Paul used the feminine προστάτις in
this last sense, meaning that Phoebe stood at the head of the
church at Cenchreae, is a totally unlikely hypothesis. Such
use of the term would contradict his views on the role of
women in the church, and would also be inconsistent with
the context of the verse. It is not because Phoebe was president that Paul asks for help on her behalf, but because she
herself had given help to many, including Paul himself. If
she had been president of the church, then Paul would have
recommended her as such. This he did not do. Instead,
he points out that she is a sister and deaconess of the church
at Cenchreae, but he asks that Phoebe be helped because she
was a προστάτις without specifying a church. Fr. M.-J.
Lagrange, in his commentary on the epistle to the Romans,
assumed that προστάτις meant protector or patron, and
proceeded with his exegesis on that basis. He believed that
Phoebe occupied the kind of position that allowed her to
take action on behalf of Christians, especially foreign Christians.[14] Accordingly, in Lagrange's opinion, those outside the
church saw Phoebe as a patron, while to those within the
church she was a "deaconess."

This exegesis of the term προστάτις as it occurs in
Romans 16:1-2 gives rise to several doubts. First, since Paul
was a Roman citizen he had no need of protection. Secondly,
we do not even know if women performed the role of patron
which Lagrange ascribes to Phoebe. I think it necessary to
modify somewhat Lagrange's exegesis. We know that Paul

---

[13]See A. Kalsbach, *Die altkirchliche einrichtung der diakonissen bis
zu ihrem Erlöschen* (Freiburg 1926); W. Bauer, *Griechisch-Deutsches
Woerterbuch* (Berlin 1952) col. 1308-9.

[14]M.-J. Lagrange, *S. Paul, Épître aux Romains* (Paris 1922) 363.

especially valued those who offered hospitality to him and to other Christians, particularly so if someone offered his house for the eucharistic gathering. Gaius is mentioned as one of the latter in this same epistle (Rm 16:23); Nympha was probably another (Col 4:15); perhaps also Philemon; and likewise Prisca and Aquila, of whom Paul speaks with special love and gratitude (Rm 16:3-5). Based on this evidence, would it not be more accurate to consider Phoebe a προστάτις in the sense that she welcomed Christians into her home, including Paul himself? This of course supposes that she assisted them whenever they were in need of anything. Therefore, her ministry was the offering of hospitality to strangers, caring for those who accepted her offer and, generally, assisting newly arrived Christians with whatever they needed. Consequently, everything that Paul says about Phoebe in 16:2 is an elaboration of the term διάκονος in 16:1. If Paul had used προστάτις in connection with Prisca and Aquila, in whose home ("house church") Christians gathered to celebrate the eucharist, then we would have had some basis for considering these persons church presidents, for the presiding officer was very often the person who had offered his home for church gatherings. All this leads us to conclude that there is no evidence of female presidents during apostolic times. Furthermore, there is no evidence of female presidents in the canonical literature prior to the second half of the fourth century, or, more precisely, before the Council of Laodicea.

Nevertheless, we do have some indirect references to support the evidence of Laodicea. These can be found not in church writings but in anti-Christian literature. Porphyrius, in his work *Against the Christians* (c. 274) vehemently disapproves of the role women played in the life of local churches. He reports that they formed a "senate" which had even been responsible for staging plays during church services.[15] Porphyrius was well acquainted with the life of Christians, so we have no basis for doubting his information, though of course he may have been inaccurate in some de-

[15] A. Harnack, *Porphyrius, "Gegen die Christen," 15 Bücher. Zeugnisse, Fragmente und Referate* (Berlin 1916) fragment 97.

tails. How should we understand the "senate" which Porphyrius mentions? Does it refer to the presbyterium, which, as
we already know, was termed the *synedrion* by St. Ignatius
of Antioch? We can assume that this "senate" was composed
of women who held a special ministry and could be thought
of as a women's presbyterium. According to this hypothesis,
the women's presbyterium would have managed the female
members of the local church and probably deliberated about
candidates for the orders of deaconesses or widows. Members of the women's presbyterium naturally must have occupied the first place in the church assembly on the same level
as presbyters. For this reason they could be called presidents,
just as the presbyters were called.

This is perhaps the most credible explanation of Porphyrius' evidence, but other explanations are not excluded, particularly since it has several faults. If in fact a special "senate"
made up of women existed, it would have meant that two
parallel bodies existed in the local church: one presbyterium
of presbyters for the male half of the congregation, and
another presbyterium of presbytides for the female half.
Consequently, we cannot exclude the possibility that the
"senate," or *synedrion,* or presbyterium, was composed not
only of presbyters but presbytides as well. In the absence of
any other facts, it is difficult to support either one of these
hypotheses decisively. This, however, is inconsequential. What
is important is the fact that the existence of presbytides as
female presidents can to some degree be substantiated in the
second half of the third century. The testimony of Porphyrius
now acquires a meaning of prime importance as background
to the testimony of the Laodicean council.

The absence of any evidence apart from the Council of
Laodicea, however, forces us to conclude that the institution
of presbytides or female presidents was not a Church-wide
phenomenon but was limited to an apparently not very sizable
circle of several local churches. Porphyrius was a native of
Palestine and evidently knew Palestinian church life quite
well, especially since he had been a Christian, or at least a
catechumen. He had traveled a great deal and had possibly
been to Asia Minor; however, we cannot be sure of this, so

we must rely on Laodicea canon 11 to tell us where female presidents existed. If they were to be found anywhere it would have been in Laodicea itself, or within the borders of Phrygia. This geographical clue is extremely important. Phrygia had been the birthplace of Montanism, which, after firmly establishing itself, had spread to neighboring provinces. We know that in Montanism women played a very important role, a role which the death of the first Montanist prophetesses did not diminish. Epiphanius recounts how processions of young girls dressed in white majestically entered Montanist gatherings to call the people to repentance. Furthermore, Epiphanius maintains that women were appointed as clergy, most likely presbyters and deacons.[16]

Although the Church resolutely fought against Montanism, its influence on the life of the catholic Church was very significant, especially in Phrygia. We can easily assume that women were appointed as presbyters in a number of churches influenced by Montanism. This could have been readily accomplished since orthodox churches had widows, deaconesses and, in some cases, presbytides as the eldest of the widows. We already know that according to the *Testament of our Lord Jesus Christ* these presbytides occupied the place immediately behind the presbyters. It was only necessary to move them ahead slightly to place them together with the presbyters. This could have happened by way of imitation, or with the intention of keeping the more active women within the orthodox Church—for if they had found no use for their activism within the orthodox churches, these women may well have been drawn away by the Montanist preachers. Finally, *oikonomia* may at first have prompted church authorities not to prevent female presidents from serving as presbyters in those Montanist communities which had come back to the catholic Church. In the second half of the fourth century, then, members of the Laodicean council from other provinces were able to call the council's attention to the existence of female presidents—something their own churches did not have—and to insist that they not be appointed in the future.

Porphyrius, consciously or unconsciously, could of course

---

[16]*Panarion* 49:2.

have easily confused orthodox churches with Montanist communities. It is probable that the Montanists more readily drew
the attention of pagans—particularly polemists, since they gave
them more ammunition for criticizing Christianity. It is also
possible that Lucian's satire of Christianity, *On the Death of
Peregrinus,* depicts life in a Montanist and not an orthodox
community. According to Lucian, after Peregrinus became a
Christian he was made a "physiarch," *synagogeus* and
prophet among the Christians. According to Labriole, we
cannot be certain that the first two terms (physiarch and
"leader of the assembly") can be equated with "bishop."[17] We
can eliminate this doubt if we assume that Lucian is speaking
not about an orthodox but a Montanist community, where
these terms would have been completely appropriate. The
third term (prophet) is even more in keeping with a Montanist community rather than an orthodox church. That a prophet
would have stood at the head of an orthodox church in the
second half of the second century is almost inconceivable.

The Montanist roots of "female presidents" would appear
to be unquestionable. Of course, this is a hypothesis, but it is
a very credible one. In any case, it explains the reference we
could not otherwise understand in the eleventh canon of
Laodicea. Aside from this, it also explains the even more
curious fact that we learn nothing about these persons from
other church documents. Female presidents first appeared not
in orthodox churches but in Montanist communities.[18] One
way or another, they made their way into several orthodox
churches within a very limited geographical circle.

Church conscience refused to accept a women's ministry
of presbyters because it entailed the danger of allowing women
to perform sacraments, a function that belonged to presbyters
in the second half of the third century. This danger was quite
real. Several indirect references indicate that deaconesses and
widows aspired to widen their liturgical functions, which had
been limited entirely to giving assistance when bishops or
priests celebrated baptisms. The compiler of the *Apostolic
Constitutions* remarks: "The appointment of women priests

[17]P. de Labriolle, *La réaction païenne* (Paris 1934) 104.
[18]See the *Reallexikon für Antike und Christentum* 3:924.

to stand before goddesses is a delusion of Hellenic godless-
ness and not a decree of Christ." He adds, referring to women
performing baptisms: "If it would have been fitting to be
baptized by women, then of course the Lord would have been
baptized by his mother and not by John; or, having sent us
out to baptize, he would have sent women as well. But he
never commanded any such thing . . ."[19] In the pseudo-
decretals of Pope Sotirius (166-174), deaconesses are forbidden to touch the sacred vessels or cense the altar, as the
vestal virgins had done. The fact that this decretal is spurious
and obviously does not date from the second half of the second century is not important for us; what is important is the
subject. This decree of the Western Church is echoed in an
even later document of the Eastern Church. The *Alphabetical
Syntagma* of Matthew Blastares (fourteenth century) includes
the following reference: "Deaconesses are forbidden to cense
before the all-pure mysteries, or to take in their hands the
sacramental fans, which is the deacon's function."[20] These
instructions are evidence that deaconesses tended to totally
identify their ministry with the ministry of deacons; also, they
show that perhaps in several locales deaconesses actually
usurped the ministry of deacons. We can see these same
tendencies among deaconesses in regard to teaching. While
church authorities did not forbid deaconesses to teach in
special circumstances, such as in preparing women cate-
chumens, they were not allowed to teach during the church
assembly: "We do not allow women to teach in church, but
only to pray and listen to the teachers."[21]

If deaconesses sought to take on the full ministry of
deacons, and even to expand it, then how much greater would
the danger have been if the church authorities had recognized
the ministry of women presbyters who had left Montanism.
They, in a sense, had even more right than deaconesses to
lay claim to performing sacraments and teaching. While the
church from the very start admitted women to social work
in the widest sense of that word, it firmly refused to recog-

[19]*Apostolic Constitutions* 3:9.
[20]*Alphabetical Syntagma*, chapter 11, letter Γ.
[21]*Apostolic Constitutions* 3:6.

nize in them a priestly dignity, which included teaching in
the church assembly. In the words of Epiphanius of Cyprus,
"The Church never appointed women presbyters or priests."[22]

[22]*Panarion* 79:4.

The Characteristics and Nature of the Order of the Deaconess

BY KYRIAKI KARIDOYANES FITZGERALD*

The question of ordaining women to the holy priesthood is a theological one that has already been addressed within the life of the Orthodox Christian Church.[1] Reflecting the reality of the divine self-disclosure, Orthodox Christianity sees the Church, the world and humanity differently from other religions. Therefore, from the Orthodox perspective, the questions related to ministry in the Church must be understood in terms of our participation in the life of the triune God, and not solely in social or even political terms. Present trends within Western Christianity and society, as well as legitimate pastoral needs, however, compel us to reflect more deeply on the nature of ministry within the life of the Church. Such reflection should examine the nature of both ordained and nonordained ministries as they have existed within the Orthodox Church.

*Kyriaki Karidoyanes FitzGerald is a recent graduate of Holy Cross Greek Orthodox School of Theology in Brookline, Mass. She has studied at the Theological Faculty of the University of Thessaloniki and is now completing her doctorate at Boston University. Mrs. Karidoyanes is an active participant in meetings on women in the Church.

[1]See John Karmiris, Ἡ Θέσις καὶ ἡ Διακονία τῶν Γυναικῶν ἐν τῇ Ὀρθοδόξῳ Ἐκκλησίᾳ (Athens 1978) esp. 7-46; Maximos Aghiorgoussis, *Women Priests?* (Brookline, Mass.: Holy Cross Greek Orthodox Press, 1976); Thomas FitzGerald, "An Orthodox View on the Ordination Question," *The Living Church* (February 8, 1976) 9-14; and, of course, the articles in the pesent volume.

Our purpose is to outline some of the characteristics of one of these ministries—the order of the deaconess. We will describe the major practical aspect of her ministry and discuss the spirit behind it. While reference will be made to a number of documents dating from the first millennium, our primary sources will be the *Syriac Didascalia* and the *Apostolic Constitutions,* which date from the third and fourth centuries, respectively. While no extant document gives a thorough analysis of the variety of ministries that were exercised in the early Church, these documents give us the most complete insights into the organization of the ecclesial ministries of that period and are consistent with church practice.

Early Development

It is difficult to outline the exact historical development of the order of the deaconess, as the documents that mention the deaconess are not comprehensive, and there were differing practices in the early Church. While the order flourished in the East until the Middle Ages, it was generally discouraged in the West and never received the same prominence and recognition as it did in the East.[2] While we might wish there were more uniformity, the fact remains that the responsibilities, position and qualifications of the deaconess differed from place to place and from period to period. There was no established and universal practice.

We do know that the order can trace its origins to the time of the New Testament. St. Phoebe is mentioned by St. Paul in his epistle to the Romans as a *diakonos* of the church of Cenchreae.

> I commend to you our sister Phoebe, a deaconess [διάκονον] of the church at Cenchreae, that you may receive her in the Lord as befits the saints, and help her in whatever she may require from you, for she has been a helper of many and of myself as well. (Rm 16:1-2)

[2]Mary McKenna, *Women of the Church* (New York: J.P. Kennedy and Sons, 1967) 121.

While some may argue that the term *diakonos* should be understood as helper or minister, the subsequent tradition does not support that position. In the case of Phoebe, the title refers to a specific service and not to service in general. Thus, Origen says:

This text [Rm 16:1-2] teaches with the authority of the Apostle that even women are instituted deacons in the Church. This was the function which was exercised in the church of Cenchreae by Phoebe, who was the object of high praise and recommendation by Paul. He enumerated her outstanding works; she assisted everyone, he said—i.e., she helped them in their needs—she also helped me in my needs and my apostolic work with a perfect devotion. I readily compare her action with the hospitality of Lot, who never failed to welcome guests who presented themselves, and thereby deserved one day to grant his hospitality to angels. In the same manner, likewise, Abraham, who always came forward to greet his guests, deserved to have the Lord with his angels visit him and stay under his tent. Also this pious Phoebe, while giving assistance and rendering service to all, deserved to assist and to serve the Apostle himself. And thus this text teaches at the same time two things: that there are, as we have already said, women deacons in the Church, and that women, who have given assistance to so many people and who by their good works deserve to be praised by the Apostle, ought to be accepted in the diaconate. He also exhorted that those [women] who are active in good works in the Church receive likewise in return from their brethren consideration and be treated with honor, in whatever matter is necessary, even in material services.[3]

Similarly, St. John Chrysostom, in his commentary on Romans, refers to Phoebe as a deacon of the church of Cenchreae.[4] He praises Phoebe for her goodness and sanctity.

[3]*Commentary on Romans* 10:17.
[4]*Homily 30 on Romans.*

Moreover, St. John commends both men and women to imitate her. It is also important to note that St. John interprets 1 Timothy 3:11 as referring not to women in general but to women deacons. Speaking of this passage, he says:

> Some have claimed that this [passage] is said of women generally, but it is not so, for why should he [St. Paul] introduce anything about women to interfere with his subject? He is speaking of those who hold the rank of Deaconess . . . For that order is necessary and useful and honorable in the Church.[5]

Holy Tradition looks to Phoebe as the prototype of the deaconess, the first deaconess of the Church. The second of the ordination prayers to the female diaconate compares the woman being ordained to Phoebe. The prayer implores God to help her "fulfil the grace of your ministry, just as you gave the grace of your ministry to Phoebe, whom you called to the work of ministry."[6]

Another example of the significance of Phoebe is to be found on a fifth-century Byzantine tombstone on the Mount of Olives. This epitaph draws a parallel between Phoebe and the deceased deaconess. It says, "Here lies the servant and bride of Christ, Sophia the deacon [Σοφία ἡ διάκο-νος], a second Phoebe, who fell asleep in peace on the twenty-first day during the month of March."[7]

Certainly, we cannot neglect the fact that the Orthodox Church commemorates a number of women saints who were deaconesses, beginning with St. Phoebe, whom we commemorate on September 3. St. Macrina (July 19) was the sister and teacher of Sts. Basil the Great and Gregory of Nyssa. After helping raise and educate her brothers and sisters, she founded a monastery on the Iris River in Pontus. St. Nonna (August 6), wife of Gregory of Nazianzus the elder and mother of Gorgonia and Gregory the Theologian, helped

---

[5]*Homily 11 on Timothy.*
[6]See the text of the ordination service below (pp. 94-5).
[7]Evangelos Theodorou, Ἡρωΐδες τῆς Χριστιανικῆς Ἀγάπης (Athens 1949) 79.

guide her husband's conversion to Christianity. Her son, the great theologian, praises her in his writings and remembers her life of prayer and sacrifice. St. Melania (December 31) lived during the fourth century as well. The granddaughter of St. Melania the elder, after the death of her two children, she and her husband gradually gave their immense wealth to the poor and to the Church. Later, they traveled to Jerusalem, where they each became monastics, and she later founded a hospice for pilgrims and established a monastery for women. St. Melania dedicated her life to instructing her nuns, studying the Holy Scriptures and copying books. She also converted many women and men to Christianity. St. Theosebia (January 10), the wife of St. Gregory of Nyssa, was ordained a deaconess right after her husband was consecrated a bishop, and she remained with him as his sister-wife. At her funeral oration, St. Gregory the Theologian praises her as being "the boast of the Church and the blessing of our generation." St. Gorgonia (February 23) was the only daughter and eldest child of Gregory of Nazianzus. After raising her family, she was baptized and opened her house to the poor. St. Olympias (July 25) was the closest friend of St. John Chrysostom. After the untimely death of her husband, she gave her riches to the poor and founded a hospital and female monastery in Constantinople, where she served as abbess and deaconess. She was often consulted by St. John Chrysostom on ecclesial matters, and was later exiled from the city because of her loyalty to him. St. John wrote St. Olympias seventeen letters from his exile. St. Apollonia (February 9) is one of the few deaconesses who is commemorated in the Roman calendar. She was an aged deaconess in Alexandria during the third century, who was attacked by a crowd of unbelievers, had her teeth knocked out and was also threatened with fire. St. Xenia (January 24) was the only daughter of a Constantinopolitan senator of the fifth century. In order to avoid a forced marriage, she fled to Cyprus with two of her maid-servants. She was then sent to Alexandria by St. Epiphanius, where she was ordained a deaconess by Patriarch Theophilus. Later, St. Xenia founded a monastery named after St. Stephen the Deacon and Protomartyr. She was often consulted as a "spiritual mother" by many people in the towns near the monastery.[8]

The Position and Functions of the Deaconess

Of the various female ecclesiastical vocations, the deaconess holds a position that is unique in both the *Didascalia* and the *Apostolic Constitutions*. While these documents discuss the office of widow and the office of virgin, neither of these appears to have the same dignity as the order of the deaconess. Both the widow and the virgin are viewed as part of the laity and not the clergy. While both are to be honored in the assembly, neither engages in any aspect of public ministry apart from that expected of all Christians. While both enter their office with the blessing of the bishop and have distinct obligations, neither the widows nor the virgins are viewed as being ordained.

The deaconess, on the other hand, is viewed quite differently. Her responsibilities are discussed within the same context as the deacon, the presbyter and the bishop in the *Didascalia*,[9] while in the *Apostolic Constitutions* her responsibilities are discussed together with those of the subdeacon and doorkeeper.[10] Clearly, this reflects some ambiguity with regard to the exact position of the deaconess within the ecclesiastical hierarchy. Yet, it is important to note that the deaconess is not discussed within the context of the widows and the virgins. Although the widows and virgins receive the blessing of the bishop, they are considered to be laypersons. The deaconess, however, is ranked among the clergy in both documents.

[8]Elisabeth Behr-Sigel, "The Meaning of the Participation of Women in the Life of the Church," *Orthodox Women: Their Role and Participation in the Orthodox Church*, eds. Constance Tarasar and Irina Kirillova (Geneva: World Council of Churches, 1977) 17-29; Victor Matheou, ed., Ὁ Μέγας Συναξαριστὴς τῆς Ὀρθοδόξου Ἐκκλησίας (Attica, Greece 1956); McKenna, 83-93; Theodorou, Ἡρωΐδες, 62-80.

[9]*Syriac Didascalia* 9:2:28, following the *Didascalia Apostolorum*, ed. Robert Connolly (Oxford 1929). See also Johannes Quasten, *Patrology*, vol. 2 (Utrecht 1953) 147-52.

[10]*Apostolic Constitutions* 2:4:25.

Further support for this observation can be found in the ecclesiastical and the civil legislation of approximately the same period. Evangelos Theodorou maintains that the Byzantine legislation consistently includes the deaconess within the ranks of the clergy and not the laity. Canon 15 of Chalcedon, for example, notes that deaconesses should not be ordained (χειροτονεῖσθαι) until the age of forty. Similarly, the Novels of Justinian always count the deaconess as part of the clergy. The famous third novel, for example, stipulates the number of clerics serving at Hagia Sophia. Among the 425 clergy, there are supposed to be forty deaconesses. In the sixth novel, moreover, the emperor speaks of the "hierosyne" of the deaconess.[11]

Both the *Didascalia* and the *Constitutions* agree that the primary function of the deaconess was to assist the bishop in baptizing women.[12] But on closer inspection it appears that her ministry encompassed much more. According to the *Didascalia,* much of the ministry of the deaconess to women paralleled the ministry of the deacon to men. Both were assistants to the bishop and each had to answer to him.[13] The deaconess also exercised other significant functions associated with the liturgical services. She exchanged the kiss of peace with the women in the assembly during the eucharist. Moreover, she was the keeper of the doors, responsible for the female part of the congregation. It was her responsibility to keep the women in order and to receive female visitors into the worshiping community.[14] Acting under the direction of the bishop, who was the father of the community, the deaconess was the leader of the female segment of the congregation. It is interesting to note that no woman was permitted to speak to the bishop, or even the deacon, without first speaking to the deaconess.[15]

[11]Evangelos Theodorou, Ἡ "Χειροτονία" ἢ "Χειροθεσία" τῶν Διακονισσῶν (Athens 1954) 44.
[12]*Didascalia* 16:3:12; *Apostolic Constitutions* 3:2:15-6.
[13]*Didascalia* 16:3:12.
[14]*Apostolic Constitutions* 2:7:57-8.
[15]*Apostolic Constitutions* 2:4:26. The deaconess also took communion to women who were ill and otherwise could not come to the eucharist. See the *Testamentum Domini Nostri Jesu Christi* 2:20:7.

The deaconess had important catechetical and charitable responsibilities as well. She was expected to instruct the newly baptized adult Christian women on how to live a holy and pure life, becoming in effect their spiritual mother.[16] The deaconess distributed the charitable donations of the Church to the women in the congregation, including the widows.[17] She visited and ministered to the sick. The deaconess was sent by the bishop into the homes of Christian women living in heathen households in order to minister to them.[18] What specific functions this ministry entailed, however, are not elaborated, but we do know that both documents affirm the fact that the deaconess was required to do many things.[19] And it was expected of the deaconess to minister to women just as a deacon would minister to men outside of the liturgical setting.[20]

The *Didascalia* draws a parallel between the deaconess and the pious women who were associated with our Lord. After identifying some of the activities of the deaconess, the *Didascalia* states:

> For this cause we say that the ministry of a woman deacon is especially needful and important. For our Lord and Savior also was ministered unto by women ministers, Mary Magdalene and Mary, the daughter of James and the mother of Jose, and the mother of the sons of Zebedee, with other women besides.

Then, speaking to the bishop, the text says: "And you also have need of the ministry of a deaconess for many things."[21]

Both the *Didascalia* and the *Apostolic Constitutions* clearly express the fact that the ordained ministry exists within the life of the Church.[22] As a consequence of this, every order of ministry has qualifications and limitations that are fixed by

----

[16]*Didascalia* 16:3:12.
[17]*Apostolic Constitutions* 3:1:14.
[18]*Didascalia* 16:3:12-3.
[19]*Didascalia* 16:3:12; *Apostolic Constitutions* 3:1:15.
[20]*Didascalia* 16:3:13.
[21]*Didascalia* 16:3:12.
[22]*Didascalia* 9:2:26; *Apostolic Constitutions* 2:4:26.

the Church. The deaconess, according to the *Apostolic Constitutions,* must be faithful and holy. With the deacon, the deaconess must be "ready to carry messages, to travel about, to minister and to serve."[23] Like the deacon, the deaconess must know her proper place and must not be ashamed to minister to those who are in need. The hallmark of the order is loving service to others.[24]

Both male and female deacons are assistants of the bishop and are chosen by him from within the community and ordained by him for the service of the community.[25] However, there is in the documents a clear differentiation between the male and the female deacon. One is tempted to say the order of the diaconate exists in two modes, a male mode and a female mode. While many of the responsibilities of the deaconess and the deacon are similar, they are not interchangeable. Both the enumeration of responsibilities and the ordination prayers bear witness to the fact that men and women are different. Consequently, the responsibilities of the deaconess are not as extensive as those of the deacon. The deaconess, for example, does not assist at the eucharist, as does the deacon. Although both documents instruct the faithful to honor the deaconess as a type of the Holy Spirit, she does not engage in any task that is priestly.[26] In delineating the responsibilities of the male and female deacon, the *Didascalia* and *Apostolic Constitutions* reflect the fact that sexuality is neither irrelevant nor inconsequential.

The *Apostolic Constitutions* provide us with a prayer for the ordination of a deaconess, contained in the text after the ordination prayer for the deacon and before the prayer for the subdeacon. The style of the prayer is very similar to the ordination prayer of the deacon, and the content of the prayer contains references to women of the Old Testament and to the Theotokos. The text says:

O Eternal God, the Father of Our Lord Jesus Christ,

[23]*Apostolic Constitutions* 3:1:15.
[24]*Apostolic Constitutions* 3:2:19.
[25]*Didascalia* 16:3:12.
[26]*Apostolic Constitutions* 8:3:28.

the Creator of man and of woman, who did replenish
with the Spirit Miriam, and Deborah, and Anna,
and Huldah; who did not disdain that your only-
begotten Son should be born of a woman; who also in
the tabernacle of the testimony, and in the temple, did
ordain women to be keepers of your holy gates, look
down now upon this your servant, who is to be ordained to the office of deaconess, and grant her your
Holy Spirit, and "cleanse her from all defilement of
flesh and spirit," that she may worthily discharge the
work which is committed to her to your glory, and the
praise of your Christ, with whom glory and adoration
be to you and the Holy Spirit for ever. Amen.[27]

The Ordination Issue

Contemporary Orthodox theologians are divided in regard to the ecclesiastical position the deaconess once had.
Should the deaconess be considered as part of the "major
orders," as was and is the deacon? Or, should she be considered as part of the "minor orders," as was and is the
subdeacon? The question hinges not primarily upon the
analysis of the functions of the deaconess, but rather upon
whether the deaconess received an ordination (χειροτονία)
or whether she received an appointment (χειροθεσία).

A principal proponent of the χειροθεσία position is
John Karmiris. Professor Karmiris emphatically affirms the
"priestly" character of the diaconate, counting the diaconate
as the third level of the ordained priesthood.[28] His position
is based upon the theological understanding that the ordained
priesthood is a special ministry of the Church, to which only
certain men are called.

Karmiris believes that there should be a clear distinction
between the deacon and the deaconess. He sees the ministry
of the deaconess as being a "clearly auxiliary institution in
the work of the Church." It is not to be confused with the

[27]*Apostolic Constitutions* 8:3:20.
[28]Karmiris, 47.

ministry of the deacon, which, according to him, is a "purely priestly ministry." For this reason, he maintains that it is abusive to consider the deaconess as being ordained. In order to support this position he cites the ambiguous canon 19 of Nicea. He also states that the term χειροτονεῖσθαι, used in canon 15 of Chalcedon, should be understood as χειροθε-τεῖσθαι. According to Karmiris, "in every instance in the ancient Church women did not in fact exercise any purely priestly ministry."[29] But while he refuses to consider the deaconess as having been ordained, he very much affirms the various ministries that were performed by the deaconess within the life of the Church.[30]

Karmiris discusses at length the fact that women were valuable coworkers of the apostles in the task of spreading the Christian faith.[31] He affirms, furthermore, that this activity of women has continued through the ages. He says that women "are equal members of the body of Christ."

> . . . women have an equal place, the same duties and rights in the Church as do men, performing an equally serious and accountable function in it, however different from the sacerdotal. . . . Women are complete and conscious and active members of the Church, having the same mission and responsibility both within and through the Church as do men, with the only difference being that they are excluded from the priesthood.[32]

Karmiris is a proponent of the ministry of laywomen in the Church. He reminds us that the women in the Bible and others in subsequent generations developed a vibrant missionary activity. Some of these women were even canonized as "Equal to the Apostles." This fact "gives force to the general

[29]Ibid., 47-9.
[30]Ibid., 48-50.
[31]Ibid., 50. The scope of Professor Karmiris' study concerns the ministry of women in the Church in general. While he focuses considerable attention on the deaconess, his primary concern is to identify the many ways in which women have served the Church.
[32]Karmiris, 13.

spiritual priesthood of the laity and the beginning of the
unity and equality of the members of the body of the Church."
He goes on to say that this gives correspondingly greater
opportunities for the contemporary Orthodox woman to serve
the Church.[33]

A strong opponent of "clericalism," this distinguished lay
theologian is especially sensitive to the important responsibilities and ministries that can be exercised by laymen and
women. He very much recognizes "the essential equality
among all of the members." Furthermore, he says that "all
of the members of the body of the Church are equal and
equally respected by each other, being different only according
to the reception of the various charisms." He maintains that
the "differentiation of the charisms of the Holy Spirit among
the members of the body of the Church is not essential
[ὀντολογική], but functional [λειτουργική]."[34]

A proponent of the χειροτονία position is Dr. Evangelos
Theodorou. He reaches the conclusion that deaconesses receive a genuine ordination after a thorough examination of
early Christian and Byzantine writings, legislation and liturgical texts. Fundamental to his conclusion is the service for
the ordination of the deaconess, which dates from the Middle
Ages. After his study of the texts, he concludes that the
ordination was a genuine ordination, and the term χειροτονία should be used to describe the setting-apart of the
deaconess. For example, Theodorou observes that the service
takes place *during* the eucharist, after the epiclesis, as is
characteristic of ordinations for the higher clergy. The ordination takes place within the sanctuary, before the holy altar.
The service begins at the same time as the ordination of the
deacon, and is carried out in the same way, with only a few
notable changes.[35] The deaconess, like the deacon, received
the orarion after being ordained and took holy communion

---

[33]Ibid., 21-2.
[34]Ibid., 26-7.
[35]For example, during the ordination, the deaconess stands, rather than
kneel on one knee as does the deacon. Neither does the deaconess take the
sacrament out to the congregation for the faithful to receive communion, as
does the deacon. Instead, the deaconess replaces the chalice by herself upon
the altar.

at the altar. Theodorou believes that all of this signifies that she was ordained.[36]

Theodorou affirms that the deaconess performed a number of valuable liturgical, catechetical and charitable functions. He discusses the responsibilities of the deaconess that are reported in the *Didascalia* and the *Apostolic Constitutions*. But, more than this, he also discusses the references to the deaconess that are scattered through other Christian documents. In addition to the responsibilities we have already discussed, Theodorou has identified a number of other tasks that characterized her ministry. For example, the deaconess received communion at the altar with the clergy.[37] She was also responsible for bringing holy communion to women who were ill and not able to come to the eucharist. An equally liturgical and pastoral responsibility of the deaconess was to visit homes of Christian women who had died. Here, she also assisted in the preparation of the bodies and in their burial.[38]

Because of her catechetical activity, the deaconess is considered by Theodorou to be a teacher of the faith. Her actions brought many pagan women and men into the Church. She was also responsible for the religious education of the women in the congregation, including mothers and unmarried women. The deaconess also taught children and especially orphans.[39] We cannot neglect the important impact that deaconesses such as Sts. Macrina, Olympias, Xenia and Melania had upon those around them.

According to Theodorou, much of the ministry of the deaconess encompassed what we call today Christian social work. She was obliged to visit the homes of those in need. This included an outreach to those in hospitals, old-age homes, orphanages and jails.[40] Some deaconesses were entrusted with being the heads of houses for unmarried women

[36]Theodorou, Ἡ "Χειροτονία," 40-65. See the text of this service at the end of this article (pp. 93-5).
[37]Theodorou, Ἡ "Χειροτονία," 56, 63.
[38]Ibid., 91-2.
[39]Ibid., 79-80.
[40]Theodorou, Ἡρωῗδες, 57.

and houses where other deaconesses lived in community.[41]
Theodorou calls the ministry of the deaconess a "work of
love" and considers them "angels of mercy."[42]

While the deaconess received a genuine ordination, this
still did not imply that she had any "priestly" responsibilities.
Theodorou emphasizes that this was not an ordination to the
sacramental priesthood, but an ordination to *diakonia*. Its
focus was essentially *service to the Church*.[43] At no time were
women called to the ordained priesthood or admitted to it by
the Orthodox Church. Theodorou affirms that the female
diaconate was not viewed as a "step" toward the priesthood
or episcopacy. "Although deaconesses were regarded as
clergy," Theodorou maintains, "they were a special class.
There was no other female clergy, either with higher or with
lower status. Deaconesses were the only class of female
ministers in the Church." Furthermore, he states that "in the
hierarchy their status was just below that of deacons, between
the deacons and the subdeacons. They were thus a branch
of the ministry of deacons with special responsibility for
diakonia among women."[44]

Both Karmiris and Theodorou credit the rise of infant
baptism as the principal cause for the decline of the order.
The deaconess was not needed to instruct or assist at the
sacrament as before.[45] They also note that abuse of the
privileges of the order may have contributed to its decline.[46]
Both Karmiris and Theodorou agree that by the eleventh
century the deaconess was confined primarily to the monastery.
Theodorou, however, notes that there were certain exceptions
to this, even up to the end of the Byzantine era.[47]

[41]Evangelos Theodorou, "The Ministry of the Deaconess in the Greek
Orthodox Church," *The Deaconess,* World Council of Churches Studies, 4
(Geneva 1966) 29.

[42]Theodorou, Ἡ "Χειροτονία," 79.

[43]Theodorou, Ἡρωΐδες, 55-6.

[44]Theodorou, "The Ministry of the Deaconess," 27.

[45]Karmiris, 50; Theodorou, Ἡ "Χειροτονία," 36.

[46]Other scholars would add that the increased responsibilities of the lower
clergy and the added priestly responsibilities of the male diaconate also helped
weaken the position of the deaconess. See, for example, J. Davis, "Deacons,
Deaconesses and the Minor Orders in the Patristic Period," *Journal of
Ecclesiastical History* 14:1 (1969) 1-12.

[47]Theodorou, Ἡ "Χειροτονία," 36.

At the heart of the difference between Karmiris and Theodorou is the nature of the diaconate. While both recognize that the deaconess once performed invaluable service to the Church, they disagree with regard to her ecclesiastical position. As we have seen, Karmiris understands the diaconate to be the third level of the ordained priesthood, which is a ministry to which women (and most men) are not called. Although acknowledging the distinctive privileges the male diaconate held, which the female diaconate did not hold, Theodorou does not see the diaconal ordination as an ordination to the priesthood—it is an ordination of ministry (*diakonia*) to the Church. According to this perspective, the diaconate is an order of ordained ministry that has an integrity and a meaning in and of itself.

Efforts to Restore the Female Diaconate

The issue of reviving the order of the deaconess has been seriously considered several times since the late nineteenth century. Not long after the death of Tsar Nicholas I in 1855, the Grand Duchess Elena Pavlovna, his sister, initiated efforts to revive the order of the deaconess in Russia. Acting on her behalf, Fr. Aleksandr Gumilevsky published a proposed rule for a community of deaconesses in 1860. This effort continued through the decade, until the death of Fr. Aleksandr.[48] The effort was resumed in 1905-1906. Among the supporters of the reactivation of the order were the abbess, Mother Ekaterina of Lesna; Bishop Stefan of Mogilev; Protopresbyter Aleksii Maltsev, the Russian chaplain of Berlin; and Bishop Evlogy, who later became Metropolitan of Volhynia and subsequently the exarch of the Ecumenical Patriarchate for Russian parishes in Western Europe. The efforts were continued by the Grand Duchess Elizaveta Fedorovna, whose proposal was seriously considered by the Holy Synod. Although no action was taken, she founded the Martha-Mary Monastic Community in Moscow. This was a monastic-nursing

---

[48]Sergei Hackel, "Mother Maria Skobtsova: Deaconess Manquée?" *Eastern Churches Review* 1:13 (1967) 265.

community in which she served as abbess. She and other members of her community were martyred during the Bolshevik Revolution.[49]

Similar efforts to revive the order of the deaconess also occurred in Greece. For example, St. Nektarios ordained a nun into the diaconate on Pentecost Sunday in 1911. Theodorou relates that the ordination took place

> during the Divine Liturgy with the laying on of hands, following the same order of prayers as the ordination of the deacon, including the prayer of the bishop saying aloud, "the Divine Grace . . ." The woman who was ordained wore a sticharion to about the waist, but not reaching the feet, with the diaconal orarion and diaconal cuffs. This same woman, who later became the abbess, accepted another deaconess, who was also ordained by St. Nektarios, into the monastery. Because certain people were scandalized with her "ordination," St. Nektarios gave an explanation to the then Archbishop of Athens, Theoklitos, emphasizing that the action of appointing them probably had more characteristics similar to that of the subdeacon and that they were needed by the monastery, especially during the absence of ordained clergymen.[50]

A few years later, Archbishop Chrysostomos of Athens appointed "monastic 'deaconesses,' who were nuns actually appointed to the subdiaconate." They had the right, according to Theodorou, to "wear the diaconal orarion, cense, decorate the holy sanctuary and, when an ordained clergyman was not present, to read the gospel pericopes during the divine services and to bring the presanctified holy gifts to the nuns who were ill."[51] Writing in the year 1954, Theodorou states that at that time there were a few monasteries in Greece where certain nuns had been ordained as deaconesses.

More recently, this issue was seriously discussed at the

[49]Ibid., 265-6.
[50]Theodorou, Ἡ "Χειροτονία," 96.
[51]Ibid.

Consultation on the Role and Participation of Women in the Orthodox Church, held in Agapia, Romania, during September 1976. It was recommended that "the office of the deaconess be studied and considered for 'reactivation' in churches where the needs of society could be met more effectively by such a service."[52] A similar conference, sponsored by SYNDESMOS, was held at St. Vladimir's Orthodox Theological Seminary in New York during the summer of 1980.

In the year 1952, the Church of Greece, through the Society of the Apostolic Diakonia, established a school for "lay" deaconesses in Athens. The candidates for study must already have theological degrees from the School of Theology of the Universities of Athens or Thessaloniki. The curriculum includes more advanced studies in theology, social sciences and social work. Theodorou maintains that:

> The purpose of this College is to train deaconesses and social workers of the Church of Greece to become direct assistants to pastors in carrying out their pastoral work in families and to undertake social welfare work in accordance with the Orthodox Church . . . they are working in parishes of the Archbishopric of Athens as lay deaconesses; they have not been ordained and do not wear a uniform. It is hoped that in the future the Church of Greece will be able to have ordained deaconesses not only in convents but in parishes also.[53]

Conclusion

Clearly, more serious thought has to be applied to the study of the true nature of the diaconate.[54] Since the time of the *Didascalia,* the priestly-liturgical responsibilities of the

---

[52]*Orthodox Women,* 50. The same report also emphasized that the character of the ministry of the deaconess concerned diakonia, and not "priestly" ministry. It further stated that "the office of the deaconess is distinct and is not new, nor can it be considered as a 'first step' to the ordained priesthood."

[53]Theodorou, "The Ministry of the Deaconess," 30.

[54]For an interesting discussion on the nature of the diaconate, see Louis Bouyer, *Women in the Church* (San Francisco: Ignatius Press, 1979) 82-7.

male diaconate have gradually increased through the centuries. However, although some male deacons may be called to pass to the order of the presbyterate and the episcopacy, the diaconate is not necessarily a "stepping stone" to higher orders. Unfortunately, the deacon is frequently viewed as an incomplete priest. This attitude is especially prevalent in many Orthodox communities in America where there is a dire need for priests.

Currently, the functions that remain for the deacon are usually only liturgical, although there are some signs of progress in recognizing the full potential of the order.[55] To separate the male deacon from working in *both* liturgical and ministerial functions is unnatural to the life of the Church. Similarly, should the order of the female deacon be revived, this fact would apply as well, "in so far as it is fitting" to her ministry. The diaconate is very much a vital part of the mission of the Church, and yet, as a recent statement of the World Council of Churches has said:

> [if it] is to be rightly understood and practiced, it must be seen in its indissoluble connection with the life of the Body of Christ. It may never be considered apart from worship and proclamation. What is expressed in words by preaching must be attested in deeds by active service; as the congregation praises God in worship and is renewed through sharing in God's work, it is equipped for new service. The relationship between worship and works of love must be especially emphasized.[56]

The order of the deaconess is very much within the memory and consciousness of the Church. Since the time of the apostles, the order has been one of the many ways in which women have followed the Lord and have contributed to the well-being of the Church. Consistent with the Orthodox understanding of the triune God and of the Church, the

[55]George Khodr, "The Diaconate in the Orthodox Church," *The Ministry of Deacons*, World Council of Churches Studies, 2 (Geneva 1965) 40.
[56]*The Deaconess*, 10.

responsibilities of the deaconess have neither impinged upon the character of the ordained priesthood nor diminished the legitimate distinctions between and the charisms of masculinity and femininity. As the example of the saints so clearly demonstrates, our Orthodox tradition bears a viable and valuable witness to the world of the many ways in which women have served the Lord and his Church. The order of the deaconess has been an important and significant one. And could not the Church in certain places benefit once again from this ministry of love and service?

The Ordination Rite of the Byzantine Deaconess

Because of the significance of the service of ordination of the deaconess, we present a translation of the text included in Theodorou's study ('H "Χειροτονία," 55-6). This service dates from the eighth-tenth centuries and is taken from the Barberion codex and the Bessarianos codex.

After the holy oblation is made, before the opening of the royal gates and before the deacon says "Having commemorated all the saints . . ." she who is to be ordained [ἡ μέλλουσα χειροτονεῖσθαι] is brought before the hierarch, and he recites:

The divine grace . . . (which always heals that which is infirm and completes that which is wanting, ordains N. to the order of deaconess. Let us pray for her, that the grace of the Holy Spirit may come upon her).

Meanwhile, she bows her head and the bishop places his hand on her head. He makes the sign of the cross three times and says the following prayer:

O God, the Holy and the Almighty, who has blessed woman through the birth in the flesh of your only-begotten Son and our God from the Virgin; and has given the grace and visitation of the Holy Spirit not to men only, but to women as well; look now, Lord, upon this your servant and call her to the work of your ministry

[εἰς τὸ ἔργον τῆς διακονίας σου]. Send down upon
her the rich gift of your Holy Spirit. Preserve her in your
Orthodox faith, that she may fulfil her ministry in blame-
less conduct according to what is well pleasing to you.
For to you (are due all honor, glory and worship, to the
Father, and to the Son and to the Holy Spirit). Amen.

After the "Amen" the deacon recites the following litany:

In peace let us pray to the Lord.
For the peace from above and for the salvation of our
souls, let us pray to the Lord.
For the peace of the whole world, let us pray to the Lord.
For our archbishop N. and for his priesthood, assistance,
maintenance, peace, health, salvation and the work of
his hands, let us pray to the Lord.
For she who is now ordained deaconess and for her
salvation, let us pray to the Lord.
That God, who loves mankind, will grant her a spotless
and blameless ministry, let us pray to the Lord.
For our pious and God-favored emperor, (let us pray to
the Lord).
For our deliverance (from all tribulation, wrath, danger
and necessity, let us pray to the Lord).
Help us, save us, (have mercy upon us and keep us, O
God, by your grace).

*And while the deacon is repeating the litany, the bishop, still
keeping his hand in the same position upon the head of the
woman being ordained, says the following prayer:*

O Lord and Master, who did not reject women who were
willing to offer themselves, in so far as it is fitting, to
minister in your holy houses, but who accepts them into
the rank of ministers [ἐν τάξει λειτουργῶν], grant
the grace of your Holy Spirit also to this your servant,
who desires to offer herself to you and to fulfil the grace
of your ministry, just as you gave the grace of your
ministry [χάριν τῆς διακονίας σου] to Phoebe, whom

you called to the work of ministry [ἔργον τῆς λει-τουργίας]. O God, grant that she may blamelessly remain in your holy temples, diligent in her proper and prudent conduct. And prove your servant perfect, so that she, standing at the judgment seat of Christ [τῷ βή-ματι τοῦ Χριστοῦ], may worthily receive the reward for her good conduct. Through the mercy and love of mankind of your only-begotten Son, with whom you are blessed, (together with your all-holy, good and lifegiving Spirit, now and ever and unto ages of ages. Amen).

After the "Amen," he puts the diaconal orarion on her neck under the omophorion, bringing the two ends forward. The deacon then stands on the ambon and says:

Having commemorated all the saints, etc.

After she has communed of the holy body and holy blood, the archbishop gives her the holy chalice, which she accepts and replaces on the holy altar.

On the Male Character of
Christian Priesthood

By Thomas Hopko*

The following considerations are presented as an attempt
to give theological and spiritual reasons why only some male
members of the Christian Church may be ordained to her
sacramental priesthood. I frankly admit that the ideas presented here are not sufficiently developed. The issue is a new
one and is complicated by many factors. There are no specific
sources dealing with it in church tradition, where the question
is not treated even in the most rudimentary form. There is
only the fact that while the orthodox, catholic Church has
known women saints, martyrs, prophets, missionaries, monastics and secular rulers, even honoring some, such as Mary
Magdalene, with the title "equal to the apostles," the Church
has never had women bishops or presbyters.[1]

The question presented is this: Is there some theological
and spiritual reason why the Church has ordained only certain
of her male members to the sacramental offices of bishop and
presbyter? Or is this merely a fact without reason, or perhaps
with many reasons that are not theologically and spiritually

*Thomas Hopko is Assistant Professor of Dogmatic Theology at St. Vladi-
mir's Seminary. A parish priest for twenty years and a member of the Faith
and Order Commission of the WCC, Fr. Hopko has written several popular
books on Orthodox doctrine and life. His most recent books, published by
SVS Press, include *All the Fulness of God* and *The Lenten Spring*. "On the
Male Character of Christian Priesthood" first appeared in *St. Vladimir's
Theological Quarterly* 19:3 (1975) 147-73.

[1]Among other women ἰσαπόστολοι are the martyr Thekla; Helen,
the mother of the Emperor Constantine; and Nina, the missionary who
converted the Georgians.

justified and are no longer socially and culturally acceptable? The position that I will attempt to defend in these pages is that there are theological and spiritual reasons why only certain male members may hold episcopal and presbyteral offices in the Church of orthodox, catholic tradition and faith, and that when the issue in question is contemplated in the light of the traditional faith of the Church, these reasons become clear and convincing to those who believe, even though they may remain foolish to those who want wisdom and scandalous to those who seek power (cf 1 Co 1:20-25). It is as a certain *fides quaerens intellectum* within the catholic tradition that I would like these reflections to be considered and criticized.

The Holy Trinity

The Christian faith, in its traditional orthodox, catholic expression, has always confessed the Godhead to be a Trinity of consubstantial, coequal and coeternal persons in perfect unity, confessing as well that true human life—*salvation*—consists in man's union with God the Father through the Son of God incarnate as a real man in Jesus Christ, that by the power of the Holy Spirit human beings might become by God's grace all that God is by nature.[2]

The one, true and living God is God the Father. He is the Creator of heaven and earth, the Lord of Israel, the Father of Christ. The one, true and living God is not, and according to orthodox theology cannot be, "alone" in his divinity. If he were "alone" he would not be God, for his very divine perfection is such that he has with himself—eternally and essentially, by nature and not by decision, by his being and not by deliberative choice—his only-begotten Son, also called his personal Logos and Image, and his Holy Spirit, who is the hypostatic personification of his divine activity and life. The Godhead is a Trinity of divine, eternal, essentially existing persons who are not simply "one" but a "union," who are

[2]See V. Lossky, *The Mystical Theology of the Eastern Church* (Crestwood, N.Y.: SVS Press, 1976) 114-28.

not simply a "unity" but a "community": the Father and the
Son and the Holy Spirit.[3]

The Image and Likeness of God

According to the same orthodox, catholic faith, humanity
is created in the image and according to the likeness of
divinity. Human nature is the created expression of the divine
nature of God the Father, Son and Holy Spirit. The multipersonal, multihypostatic character of human being and life
is the created manifestation and reflection of the trinitarian
character of God. Humanity, therefore, like divinity, is a
community of coequal, coessential persons united together in
exactly the same nature, whose essential spiritual freedom
makes it reflective and expressive of God, but whose creaturely
character—its open-ended temporality, incompleteness and
lack of "fulness"—binds it together in an unending process
of growth and development in "deification": becoming
through gracious communion with God in freedom all that
God is by nature in the superabundant fulness of his inex-
haustible and infinite trinitarian being and life.[4]

[3]See Lossky, *Mystical Theology*, 44-66; J. Meyendorff, *Byzantine Theology*
(New York: Fordham, 1974) 180-9; S. Verhovskoy, *God and Man* (in
Russian, New York: Chekhov, 1956) 360-95. In general, in patristic theology,
to be a perfect "union of many" is considered superior to being an isolated,
undifferentiated "one." This view applies to divine as well as human being
and life.

[4]See J. Daniélou and H. Musurillo, *From Glory to Glory: Texts from
Gregory of Nyssa's Mystical Writings* (New York: Scribners, 1961) 46-
71; L. Thunberg, *Microcosm and Mediator: The Theological Anthropology
of Maximus the Confessor* (Lund: C.W.K. Gleerup, 1965) 52-67, 352-465.
What is not developed by Gregory and Maximus in their view of the unending
movement of the process of human deification is its application to human
interpersonal and *communal* relationships, the concentration being on the
inner spiritual life of the soul, and, in Maximus, on cosmological issues.
Also, their views on human sexuality are at best unclear and at worst
incompatible with the biblical and sacramental witness of the Church and
her dogmatic and canonical tradition, since they both see physical sexual
reproduction, if not sexual being itself, as created in view of man's fall
into sin. The interpretation of Maximus, however, which claims that he
teaches a final androgyny is, in my opinion, incorrect, or at least highly
debatable. I base my opinion on his doctrine that the divisions (διαιρέσεις)
to be overcome by human spiritual meditation and growth in deification do

If it has not been specifically explicated and articulated in the past, it is the present task to show clearly that human community, as the created epiphany of the uncreated Trinity, is made male and female so that it can realize and achieve the divine life given to it by its uncreated Archetype. The fact that human nature, enhypostasized in a multitude of human persons, is created by God as male and female is undeniable. Why this is so, what is its meaning, and how are the sexes to interrelate to be reflective of this divine Prototype has not been sufficiently explained in Christian tradition. Perhaps the reason is that, historically, due to the actual conditions of human life, the "hour had not yet come" for this explication to be accomplished. Perhaps such an explication simply could not have been made in times past, even the "past" of our parents' generation, because the conditions of life did not require or allow it. But whatever the case, the demand for a clear and distinct explanation of the theological meaning of human sexuality is with us now, and attempts must be made to meet this demand.[5]

not destroy ontological differences (διαφοραί). If humans must overcome sexual divisions, as well as the divisions between the sensible and intelligible, heaven and earth, God and man, it does not follow that the ontological differences between these divisions are annihilated in the process. If such were the case, those who hold that Maximus teaches androgyny on the sexual level should also hold that he teaches theanthropy on the theological level, which no one claims or can claim. On this issue Thunberg is most convincing when he says, interpreting Maximus, that "man as mediator is called to annihilate divisions as διαιρέσεις on the moral level, but not as διαφοραί on the ontological level. In the latter sense, they are preserved but kept together by him" (Thunberg, 59-60). On this issue see also H. Urs von Balthasar, *Liturgie Cosmique* (Paris 1947), who epigrams his study on the theology of Maximus with the one Chalcedonian adverb: ἀσυγχύτως (unconfused)—i.e., union without ontological confusion or mixing of the members of the union.
    [5]The book by P.K. Jewett, *Man as Male and Female* (Grand Rapids: Eerdmans, 1975) is a concise analysis of human sexuality in the history of western theology. My main disagreement with the book is that its positive approach of viewing human sexuality in the light of the doctrine of humanity as *imago trinitatis* is bound by the crypto-modalistic view of the Trinity that runs through western triadology from St. Augustine to the present. Because of this, the author, an "evangelical Protestant" dialoging primarily with the theology of Karl Barth, does not see how the "partnership" between male and female he defends can be reconciled with any hierarchical view of reality; and, as such, he "rejects the traditional view which affirms the headship of the man as the bearer of the image and glory of God" (171 *et passim*). In this

Why is humanity male and female, and why (hypothetically at least) must it be male and female for it to adequately reflect within the created order the nature and life of its trinitarian Prototype through gracious communion with God? Is there an explanation for this, at least one that will be meaningful for Christian believers?

Some say that human sexuality was created by God in prevision and provision of human sinfulness and mortality and, as such, is not essential to human being and life. Others say that sexuality is itself somehow sinful and the cause of mortality. Still others would hold that God made his human creatures sexual because of the necessary and natural stages of human growth and development through which humans must evolve, in such a way that the sexual nature of human being will be transcended and overcome through biological, spiritual, social and cultural processes of human maturation.[6]

rejection, however, he fails, in my opinion, to present an image or ideal of male-female relations, or to give any sort of description about how the "partnership" between the sexes is to work in actuality. Referring to the "Creator's secret" (172) on the subject, he readily admits that he "has skirted the question of ontology in this study" (178). It is, however, precisely in the area of ontology that the "Creator's secret" is revealed, if we can refer to the scholastic dictum *agere sequitur esse:* how a being *is*, is how a being *acts.* My inclination is to accept the view of the "Creator's secret" in regard to the meaning of human sexuality and to say that this "secret" is made known in the life of the Church. On this point, I wonder if it is not pertinent to refer to another distinction in patristic theology, namely, that between *kerygma* and *dogma,* and to apply this distinction to the issue of human sexuality in general and the male priesthood in particular. Here, the point would be made that the Christian *preaching* to those "outside the Church" is Jesus as Christ and Lord, risen from the dead; and only after one enters into the mystical life of the Church and is enlightened by the gift of the Holy Spirit is one able to *understand* the "Creator's secret" about male-female relations "in the Lord." See L. Ouspensky and V. Lossky, *The Meaning of Icons* (Boston: Boston Book and Art Shop, 1969) 14-24, also 208, 215; also, for the same text, V. Lossky, *In the Image and Likeness of God* (Crestwood, N.Y.: SVS Press, 1974) 144-68.

[6]See Jewett, 23-50. At this point, a word about Galatians 3:28 and the comparison between the issues of sexuality and slavery is in order. Briefly, the radical difference between the two issues, and nationality and sexuality as well, is that while being male and female is an ontological reality in the order of creation, nationality and slavery are not. They are rather human conditions which are the result of sin. They have no ontological, theological, sacramental or eschatological substance. They have no place in the sacramental structure and life of the Church. God did not create humans to be Jews or Greeks, neither did he make them to be slaves or freemen. He did make them male

Whatever the explanation, the fact is that none of the above, which most commonly appear, are adequate to the scriptural, sacramental and canonical witness of the catholic Christian faith.

Catholic tradition, expressed primarily in the Bible, holds that "God said, 'Let us make man in our image, after our likeness' . . . so God created man in his own image and likeness, in the image of God he created him; male and female he created them. And God blessed them . . . and God saw everything that he made, and behold, it was very good" (Gn 1:26-31). The same tradition, in the "fulness" of its realization in the Christian Church, has sacramentally, spiritually, doctrinally and canonically defended and upheld the essential goodness of human sexuality and its necessity for humanity to be expressive of the divinity, in whose image it is made. If sexuality is sinful, says the catholic tradition of Christian faith, then God is the sinner.[7] If being male and female is negligible to human being and life, then God has acted unreasonably and without purpose, for he certainly could have

and female, however, and although the spiritual and moral divisions between the sexes are overcome in Christ, the ontological differences are not (see n. 4 above). Matthew 22:30 is not pertinent here because it does not say that there will be no sexual differences "in the resurrection." It rather says that "they neither marry nor are given in marriage" and are "like angels," not that they become angels. One cannot maintain that Galatians 3:28 teaches the ontological disappearance of sexual differences in Christ and reconcile this in any way with the rest of the Pauline corpus or the canonical scriptures in general—unless, of course, one defends the opinion that "So far as he [Paul] thought in terms of his Jewish background, he thought of women as subordinate . . . But so far as he thought in terms of the new insight he had gained through the revelation of God in Christ, he thought of the woman as equal to man in all things . . . [and] sensed that his view of the man-woman relationship inherited from Judaism was not altogether congruous with the gospel he preached" (Jewett, 112-3). I do not find this "solution" convincing. The solution rather has to be, in my mind, the genuine compatibility between *hierarchy* and *equality* in perfect spiritual union of human being and life in love, which I believe is the apostolic doctrine of the catholic faith witnessed in the scriptures and sacraments of the catholic Church.

[7]"God made nothing unclean, for nothing is unclean, except sin only. For that reaches the soul and defiles it. Other uncleanness is human prejudice . . . God made child-birth and the seed of copulation . . . and the fornicator is not unclean on account of the intercourse, but on account of the manner of it . . ." John Chrysostom, *Homily 3 on Titus*. See also the canons of the Council of Gangra and the Orthodox ritual of marriage.

devised some manner of human being, made in his likeness, that would reproduce itself in a way not requiring two sexes. (This, of course, presupposes that human disexuality has physical reproduction as its sole significance.) But if human sexuality is *spiritually* necessary to proper human being and life beyond the need for the biological reproduction of the species, then its reason and purpose must be discovered and disclosed.

The Meaning of Human Sexuality

If we go beyond all the biological and cultural explanations for the necessity of human sexuality—the procreation of offspring, the perpetuation of the species, the divisions of labor in preserving life, the distribution of roles for preserving social harmony—and turn to theology, I believe that we can discover reasons for the necessary existence of human sexuality that radically surpass all purely pragmatic and utilitarian purposes. These reasons are summed up, in a word, by the fact that multipersonal, disexual spiritual existence is a necessity if human nature is to partake of the nature of God and reflect divine existence in the order of creation. For whatever human beings may *do,* they *are,* in their interpersonal and communal being and life, made in the image and according to the likeness of God. And what humans must do *in community,* and not as isolated individuals, is to acquire and activate, ever more perfectly, all of the spiritual and moral attributes of God.

There are no human spiritual attributes that are not, essentially and perfectly, attributes of God.[8] If the Godhead is a Trinity of divine persons fully united in a perfect community of one being, one life, one wisdom, one truth and one love, then humanity also, within its creaturely conditions, must be —or rather, more accurately, must ever more perfectly *become* —the same. If divinity is a perfect interrelationship of many

[8]See Gregory of Nyssa, *Homily 81 on the Song of Songs;* Macarius of Egypt, *Spiritual Homilies* 17; Maximus the Confessor, *Centuries on Love* 2:52; also Thunberg, 196-216.

(three) distinctly existing persons, each with its own proper
hypostatic characteristics and properties, none existing apart
from the other and certainly not in opposition to the other,
but each realizing and expressing that mode of divine existence proper to itself in oneness of nature, being and life with
the others, so humanity, within its own creaturely possibilities,
must be the same. If the persons of the Trinity are not isolated "individuals" but persons in relation with one another,
each with its own proper manner of divine existence which
is existentially, personally and hypostatically *different* from
the others, so humanity as well, according to its own proper
form of being, must be the same.[9]

As we contemplate the Blessed Trinity as revealed to us
in the community of faith of the catholic tradition of the
Church, we see that God the Father is divine in a manner
different from the Son and the Holy Spirit, just as the Son
and the Holy Spirit are divine—in community with God the
Father and with each other—each in his own distinct and
specific way. The Father is the *principium divinitatis,* the
unique source of being and life of all that exists: of the Son
and of the Holy Spirit by his very divine nature, and of the
whole of creation by his divine decision and will.[10]

The Son is the uncreated Logos and Image of the Father,
the one by, through and for whom all things are made. He is
the "reflection of the glory of God," the "express image" of

[9]Concerning the propriety of the *three* persons of the Trinity, the theological conclusion normally reached is that the *three* "modes of existence"
(τρόποι ὑπάρξεως) are *necessary* for perfect "fulness" of being and life,
which is not *possible* for one or two "modes of existence" to complete and
realize, whereas more than three would be impossible and unnecessary. See
Lossky, *Mystical Theology,* 47; and *In the Image and Likeness of God,*
86. This has an application, I think, to human sexuality being *dual* (and
not one or more than two), since the male and female forms of human
existence find their mutual fulfilment and fulness in the "third": God. For
such a speculation, see John Chrysostom, *Homily 20 on Ephesians.* For a
summary of the traditional teaching about the hypostatic characteristics and
properties of the persons of the Trinity, see John of Damascus, *On the Orthodox Faith* 8. Concerning real "differentiation" in the Godhead, see Dionysius
the Areopagite, *On the Divine Names.*
[10]See G. Florovsky, "The Concept of Creation in Saint Athanasius,"
Studia Patristica 4, part 4, Texte und Untersuchungen, 81 (Berlin 1962) 36-57;
and "The Idea of Creation in Christian Philosophy," *The Eastern Churches
Quarterly* 7 (1949) 53-77.

the Father's "hypostasis" (Jn 1:2; Col 1:16; Heb 1:3), who "for us men and for our salvation . . . was incarnate of the Holy Spirit and the Virgin Mary and became man" (Nicene Creed). He is the Messiah of Israel who, in "human form" (Ph 2:8), was crucified under Pontius Pilate and rose from the dead on the third day, granting life to the world. He is the final Adam in human flesh (1 Co 15); the sole "high priest of our confession" (Heb 3:1); the "pastor and bishop" of our souls (1 Pt 2:25); the head of his body, the Church (Eph 1:23; Col 1:18, et al.); the husband of his "pure bride" (2 Co 11:2; Eph 5:21 ff).

The Holy Spirit is "the Lord," with the Father and the Son, the "giver [or creator] of life" (Nicene Creed). The Holy Spirit "proceeds from the Father and rests in the Son," and accomplishes all things willed by the Father and performed by the Son.[11] The Spirit is the one who inspires the law and the prophets to be and to proclaim the Word of God; who "searches the depths of God" (1 Co 2:10) and rests on Jesus, anointing him as the Christ; who dwells in all who believe, making them to be "one spirit" with God (1 Co 6:17). By the personal power of the Holy Spirit, human beings become "gods by grace" and express the spiritual attributes that belong to God.[12]

For our present purposes, we must recognize that although it is the Son who is the "image of the invisible God" (Col 1:15; 2 Co 4:4), the incarnate Lord, the last Adam, the one high priest, the pastor and bishop of the Church, its husband and head, and not the Holy Spirit, this in no way detracts from the divinity of the Spirit or degrades the Spirit as one of the consubstantial Trinity. Simply put, because the Holy Spirit is not the Father or the Son but the "third person" of the Holy Trinity, and because the Spirit does not do what the Father and the Son do, this in no way lessens the dignity and equality of the Holy Spirit as being divine. On the contrary,

[11] Cf the Orthodox Vespers of Pentecost. See also Meyendorff, 168-79, 184; and Lossky, *Mystical Theology*, 156-73.

[12] "Clothed in the radiant garments of the Spirit, we abide in God and He in us; through grace we become gods and sons of God, and are enlightened by the light of His knowledge . . ." Simeon the New Theologian, *Practical and Theological Precepts* 48.

the Father and the Son could not be divine and act as they do without the cooperation and coaction of the consubstantial Spirit—just as the Spirit's own being and action are impossible and unthinkable without the Father and the Son.

As the Father, Son and Holy Spirit do not exist or act without each other in their eternal being and action, as well as in the creation of the world and the dispensation of salvation, so, *in the order of creation,* Adam and Eve, male and female, do not and cannot exist and act without one another. As the Logos and the Holy Spirit perform and accomplish the will and the work of God in their common being and action, so human being and action, as performing and accomplishing the will and work of God, also require the two forms of human being: male and female. As there is not and cannot be the Son of God without the Holy Spirit, so there is not and cannot be Adam without Eve. Adam alone is not and cannot be "the image and glory of God" (1 Co 11:7) without Eve. He cannot be the "type of the one who was to come" (Rm 5:14)—that is, the Christ—without her who is the "mother of all living" (Gn 3:20). There must be woman if man is to be what and who he is, just as woman would not be what and who she is without man. Even if we knew nothing about how in actuality the two forms of human existence are to interrelate and interact so that humanity could live in the image and likeness of God, the very fact of human beings existing in this way should be enough for us to defend the necessity of this form of existence for human fulfilment and perfection of life.

It is the thesis of this paper that, according to the catholic tradition of the Christian faith, there is a direct analogical, symbolic and epiphanic relationship between Adam and the Son of God, and between Eve and the Spirit of God. As Adam is the *typos* of him "who was to come" as the final Adam, the "high priest of our confession" and the "pastor and bishop of our salvation," so Eve is the *typos,* as the "mother of all living," of the "life-creating" Spirit, who "proceeds from the Father and rests in the Son" as the personal power and life of all that exists, both human and divine.[13] What this means is

[13]Methodius of Olympus identifies the new Eve with the Church (see

that as in the Godhead there is and must be a union between the Son and the Holy Spirit for the Father to be eternally and divinely expressed, so *on the level of creation* there is and must be male and female so that the same God could be temporally and humanly expressed within the life of his creatures, by his divine decision and grace communicated through his Son and in his Spirit. This means as well that as the mode of being and action of the Son is different from the mode of being and action of the Holy Spirit, both eternally and essentially, as well as in the dispensation of salvation— or, more traditionally put, both according to *theologia* and *oikonomia*—so, in a similar manner, the mode of being and action of the male in creation is different from the mode of being and action of the female within the same nature of created being. More specifically, this means that as the Son and the Holy Spirit are not the same and are not interchangeable in their unique forms of their common divinity, so the male and female are not the same and are not interchangeable in the unique forms of their common humanity. This does not mean that there is something essentially belonging to divine nature that does not equally belong to the Son and the Holy Spirit, just as it does not mean that there is something essentially belonging to humanity that is not the common and equal possession of men and women. There are no "attributes" or "virtues" that the Son has that the Spirit does not have, or that Adam has which are not present in Eve. But what is true is that the *manner of realization* of the attributes and virtues common to the same nature is *different* in the different forms of natural existence; and *how* the common virtues and attributes will be personally and existentially actualized in each will be different within the unbreakable and indivisible communion of one with the other.[14]

The Banquet, or *On Virginity*), while it has been common, in the writings of Justin and Irenaeus, to see Mary as the new Eve. The point must be seen, however, of the association of Mary and the Church in Orthodox theology. See Lossky, *Mystical Theology,* 193-5; and *In the Image and Likeness of God,* 195-210. Also, A. Schmemann, "On Mariology in Orthodoxy," *Marian Library Studies, A New Series* 2 (Dayton 1970) 25-32; and "Our Lady and the Holy Spirit," *op. cit.,* Vol. 23 (1972), 69-78.

[14]Those influenced by phenomenological or psychological studies of human persons insist that there are no human psychological attributes or virtues

The Ideal of Human Relationships

After making such "theological abstractions" as those presented above, those who make them bear the burden of demonstrating how they actually apply to human life. How,

that are specifically male or female, and that the masculine and feminine spiritual traits usually presented (e.g., aggressiveness and strength in males and passivity and weakness in females) are acquired and culturally determined characteristics having nothing to do with human nature as such. While I agree that all human characteristics are found in all human persons, and must be in all, I would nevertheless contend that the *manner of realization and expression* of these same human characteristics in the two sexes is, or at least should be, different. The way, for example, that love is expressed by a father and husband will be, and ideally should be, different from the way love is expressed by a wife and mother, while the love itself is one and the same. I would say further that the various forms of the same human virtues common to all humans must have different modes of existence and expression in the human community so that humanity could be full and complete, and ever more so, in the processes of growth and communion. At this point, I would also like to make it clear that my position has nothing to do with "sophiology" or any sort of doctrine of the "divine" and "eternal feminine." There is, in my opinion, nothing "feminine" in divinity, as there is nothing "masculine." Divinity is beyond sexuality, as it is "beyond being" itself (cf Dionysius the Areopagite, *On the Divine Names* and *Mystical Theology*). My speculation is rather that sexuality is created by God as a necessary element of human being and life (like multipersonality or bodily existence) so that humanity would be able to reflect divinity *in the created order* in a manner proper to its *creaturely* existence. It is my speculation as well that we can gain insight into the proper manner of human existence in general, and human sexuality in particular, by a contemplation of the being and action of the persons of the Holy Trinity, and we can and must be instructed on this issue by the revelation of God in Christ and the Holy Spirit in the Church. God, however, is not to be thought of in human, creaturely terms. Rather, the human is to be considered in terms of God's revelation. Man is made in God's image, and not God in man's image, and earthly fathers are called fathers because of the fatherhood of God, and not vice-versa. On this point John of Damascus writes ". . . it behooves us to know that the names Fatherhood, Sonship and Procession were not applied to the Godhead by us [i.e., on the basis of our human experience and reflection] but, on the contrary, they were communicated to us by the Godhead, as the divine apostle says, 'Wherefore I bow the knee to the Father from Whom every family in heaven and on earth is named' (Ephesians 3:15). . . . For it is quite impossible to find in creation an image that will illustrate in itself exactly in all details the nature of the Holy Trinity" (*On the Orthodox Faith* 8). Athanasius also teaches this same doctrine, referring to the same apostolic text, when he says that we are made in our creaturely existence in God's pattern, and not God—the "bare idea of [whom] transcends such thoughts"—in our's (see *Against the Arians* 1:7).

in actual human relations, does such a formal "schematization" work? How does it show itself in the actual conditions of human being and behavior?

The difficulty with producing an "existential demonstration" of "theological abstractions" of any sort is always the same. The difficulty is that theological and spiritual ideals and norms always work differently in different human situations, which are not only bound and conditioned by the creaturely dimensions of time, place, social and cultural settings and actual existential possibilities, but also are infected and deformed by *sin,* defined as the wilful perversion and distortion of nature itself by its free human possessors and agents.

A "theological schema" is always an ideal, a vision, a *theoria.* In actuality, there is no time or place where one has worked to perfection among creatures, and can then be pointed to as an existential example and witness. A theological vision is always, by its very nature, a task and a call to be accepted, enacted and fulfilled as perfectly as possible, but never, in actual history, to complete perfection. In reference to the ideal vision of the interaction of male and female, the only example of its "working" that can be contemplated in actuality, at least by those who see and believe, is the relationship between Christ and the Church. But even here the quality of being an "ideal" remains. For Christ is the true Adam, the Bridegroom, and the Church is the true Eve, the bride personified in the person of Mary:[15] the company of the saved who are "full of grace" by the indwelling of the Holy Spirit and who, by the same Spirit, "hear the Word of God and keep it" (Lk 11:28).

If men and women wish to realize the ideal of their perfect manner of being within the human community, they must seek to perfect in their mutual relations the relationship between Christ and the Church. They must seek to do so within the actual conditions and possibilities of life which are uniquely theirs. They must do so as well in conflict with the temptations, questions, problems, distortions and sins, both personal and cultural, which are inevitably present in

[15]See n. 13 above.

fallen humanity, pressuring them to "miss the mark" with regard to their perfection.

Given the ideal vision, however, and the effort to realize it in life, it can generally be stated that believing males (and females as well) must first of all reject the image of the "fallen Adam," which operates so powerfully today, as the normative ideal for human "fulfilment" and "success" for both males and females. This "ideal," as summarized by the apostle John, says that human life is perfected in "the lust of the flesh and the lust of the eyes and the pride of life" (1 Jn 2:16). This "ideal" holds that human persons should live and act as self-seeking individuals who find and fulfil themselves through the satisfaction of their cravings for pleasure and power within secular society, understood as an end in itself and not as the created reflection of divine being and life.[16]

In rejecting "sinful man" as the ideal for human fulfilment, the Christian male should follow the perfect man, Christ. He should empty himself completely in love for the good of others in spirit and in truth. He should be meek and lowly, humble and poor. He should be liberated from the carnal lusts of life, "not conformed to this world" but "transformed by the renewal of . . . mind" to "prove what is the will of God, what is good, acceptable and perfect" (Rm 12:2). He should be free from all that blinds and enslaves. He should find his glory and majesty in self-emptying service in conformity with Christ, his divine image of being and

---

[16]I am convinced that the main line of the contemporary "women's movement," in rejecting any particular "feminine" ideal as its guiding principle and adopting the ideal of the identity of all human beings, without sexual differentiation, has in fact adopted the image of the "fallen male" as its norm and vision for success, achievement and fulfilment. If in the past John Chrysostom could claim that the tyrannical subjugation of women to men, which replaced a communion of equality within natural differentiation, was the result of sin, primarily covetousness, so we might claim today that the quest for equality without natural differentiation is the result of the same sin. The rejection of anything particularly "feminine" by the women's movement, at least that aspect of the movement most evidently present and popularized, is witnessed by the fact that most of the "gains" and "successes" of the movement are in terms of secular power, profit, prestige and pleasure; and, as such, are, in terms of Christian values, as unacceptable as "achievements" for males as they are for females.

action. His relations with women should be such that, by his self-sacrificing love for them, they appear not as his sinful "competitors" for earthly profits, powers and pleasures, but "in splendor, without spot or wrinkle or any such thing . . . holy and without blemish" (Eph 5:27).

Women are created and called to be men's "helpers" in their service of self-emptying love (Gn 2:18). They are to be "submissive" to men's love and service, and as such to enable and empower it—as the Holy Spirit, "incarnate by grace" in saved humanity, enables and empowers Christ himself to "fulfil" his divine ministry among his creatures. In the Christian view, it is not humiliating or degrading to be a "helper" and a "bride," just as it is not degrading to be the "servant of all" (Mt 21:27-28; 1 Tm 2:5-6). Christ is not degraded in his kenotic self-emptying, taking on the "form of a slave" (Ph 2:7). The Holy Spirit likewise is not degraded by silently, hiddenly and invisibly enabling Christ to be and to act as the Son of God and the Savior of the world, the high priest, pastor and bishop of saved humanity; and is not demeaned or defaced as a person by personally identifying himself with human persons, becoming "one spirit" with them to enable them to be Christ's body and bride. And so as well the human male is not degraded by his loving self-sacrifice, and the human female is not humiliated, demeaned or annihilated as a person by performing her natural ministry in the human community—which, without it, would not be and could not be fully human and, as such, "divine by grace."

Women must be "submitted" to men, as men themselves are "submitted" to Christ and Christ to God the Father (cf 1 Co 11:3), so that humankind may truly be human "in the Lord" (1 Co 11:11), "that the Word of God may not be discredited" (Tt 2:5): "for God has . . . called us . . . to holiness [and] whoever disregards this, disregards not man but God, who gives his Holy Spirit to you" (1 Th 4:7-8). The "submission" of women to men "in the Lord" must be active and free. It cannot be a "passive" submission, involuntarily, reluctantly and unwillingly offered. The "submission" of women to men "in the Lord" must imitate the "submission" of the Holy Spirit to Christ, which is dynamic, active and

powerful, as is Christ's submission to God and man's submission to Christ.[17] It must be a "submission" that has the
quality of a "fire cast upon the earth" (Lk 12:49), a "mighty
rushing wind" of the Spirit (Ac 2:2), which purges away
all falsehood and wickedness and "calls all to unity"[18] and not
to competitive individualism "fulfilled" through carnal "satisfaction" and secular "achievement."

This vision of the ideal in man-woman relationships is
applicable to human society in general, to all men and all
women. It has its most concrete application in the community
of marriage, in which the family is traditionally understood
as a "small church" patterned after the divine life of the
Holy Trinity and the kingdom of God, given to humans in
Christ and the Church. This same ideal vision is fundamental
and essential to the sacramental structure of the Christian
churchly community, which graciously manifests the trinitarian life of the kingdom of God within the life of this world
until the kingdom comes in power at the close of the ages,
when the "marriage of the Lamb" will be finally consummated
in Christ and his Spirit-filled bride (cf Rv 19-22).

Because of sin, the ideal vision of human relations in
general, and those between the sexes in particular, remains
a hope for humanity within the life of "this age" and a call
and a task for those who believe. Because of the distortion
and corruption of human nature and life, both individual and
personal as well as social and cultural—the "sins of the world"
—accommodations and compensations to sinful "abnormality"
must always be made in the secular realm in order for human
life to continue. Exceptions to normality, compromises and
adjustments are virtually the "rule" within human behavior
and activity outside of Christ and his kingdom revealed in
the Church, and the fact that this is so is a tragedy to be
endured and, when possible, to be healed and overcome. But

---

[17]See 1 Corinthians 11:3, 15:28. "For what if a wife be under subjection
to us? It is as a wife, as free, as equal in honor. And the Son also, though
He did become obedient to the Father, it was as the Son of God, it was as
God. For as the obedience of the Son to the Father is greater than we find
in men toward the authors of their being, so also His liberty is greater"
(John Chrysostom, *Homily 26 on 1 Corinthians*).

[18]Orthodox Hymn (Kontakion) of Pentecost.

it is not a fact which itself should be "normalized."[19]

The greatest tragedy for human being and life is when sinful abnormality is accepted as normality, when the unnatural is taken for the natural, when the "fallen" becomes the ideal, when the sin-conditioned "exception" is accepted as the "rule." The tragedy occurs when the divinely revealed vision and practice of human life as made in the image and likeness of God—whatever the "cultural conditioning" of its mode of revelation to creatures—is replaced by some other vision and practice that pretends to offer "fulfilment" to human being and life. Such an adoption of the "abnormal" for the "normal" is, I believe, what is happening today—and not only to "secular men" but also to certain Christians, who have accepted secular ideals as normative for themselves and for the life of the church community. Although modern secular "idolatries" are different from those in the past, the decomposition of human community they bring is no different from that, for example, so violently and vividly described by the apostle Paul in the first chapter of his letter to the Romans.

Human Relationships in the Church

This brings us to the life of the Christian Church in general, and to the sacrament of the priesthood in particular. Dostoevsky once said that the "vision" of Orthodox Christianity is "orthodoxy itself."[20] I begin with this remark

[19]Men must often assume the place of women, and women the place of men, when sin ruptures the normal conditions of human life. No less a "purist" than John Chrysostom orders men to follow their wives when they are wiser and better. "I would commit you to your own wives, that they may instruct you. It is true, according to Paul's law, you ought to be teachers. But since the order is reversed by sin . . . let us even take this way. . . . For the war against the devil and his powers is common to them [women] and the men, and in no respect doth the delicacy of their nature become an impediment in such conflicts, for not by bodily constitution, but by mental choice, are these struggles decided. Wherefore in many cases women have actually been more forward in the contest than men and have set up more brilliant trophies" (*Homily 7* and *Homily 8 on Matthew*).

[20]I believe the source of this saying is *The Diary of a Writer*. In any case, we can refer as well to Fr. Florovsky, who writes: "The Church is

because I understand it to mean that the very purpose of the
Christian Church, its content and reason for being, is to
constantly present to its members the vision of divine life,
which is available to human experience and normative for
human behavior whatever men's sins and historical settings.
The members of the Christian Church may stumble and fall,
they may be tempted and yield to temptation, they may be
blinded by passions and become victims of corruption, they
may be compelled by tragedy to compromise with the fallen
and sinful "facts of life," but the vision of divine perfection
given by God in Christ and the Church, by the grace of the
Holy Spirit, must remain. And the sacramental structure of
the Christian community, preserved by God's grace, guarantees that the vision remains.

The vision and experience of the kingdom of God is
preserved by the Church in its sacramental structures. Teachers
and movements come and go, theologies and pieties emerge
and pass away, parties and crusades rise and fall, but the
divine vision of human life remains in the catholic Church,
against which the "gates of hell will not prevail" (Mt 16:18).
At times, great numbers of church members, including patriarchs and popes, may lose the vision through sin—voluntarily
or involuntarily, in knowledge or in ignorance. They may
"dispute about words, which does no good," and indulge in
"stupid senseless controversies" as they "hold the form of
religion, but deny its power" and "accumulate teachers to suit
their own likings" (cf 2 Tm). But God will not be left without witnesses who hear his word and keep it, taking up the
cross—whose content of suffering is not physical pain or
social insult and mockery, but the agony of beholding "the
mystery hidden for ages in God, who created all things" and
revealed "by the Church" (Eph 3:9-10; Col 1:26), unwanted

Christ's work on earth; it is the image and abode of His blessed presence
in the world. . . . Outside the Church there is no salvation, because *salvation
is the Church*. . . . And God has revealed Himself in the Church. This is
the final Revelation, which passeth not away. Christ reveals Himself to us,
not in our isolation, but in our mutual catholicity, in our union. He reveals
Himself as the New Adam, the Head of the Church, the Head of the Body.
Therefore, humbly and trustfully we must enter the life of the Church and
try to find ourselves in it." See "Sobornost: the Catholicity of the Church,"
in *The Church of God*, ed. E. L. Mascall (London 1934) 53, 63, 73.

and unloved by those whom God loves and to whom he
has given his own divine life. This is the undeniable lesson
of biblical and church history. But whatever men do, it is the
promise of God that the Church will remain as the manifestation of divine life in the midst of the earth: the apostolic
faith, "once for all delivered to the saints" (Jude 3), proclaimed and celebrated in the liturgical assemblies of believers, whose content and form are organically and historically
inspired by the Spirit of God and whose vision of life remains
the task of the faithful for existential fulfilment in the life
of humanity.

The head of the Church is Jesus Christ, its only high priest,
pastor, teacher and bishop. The Church is Christ's "body, the
fulness of him who fills all in all" (Eph 1:23). It is, by the
Holy Spirit, Christ's bride, the new Eve of the new Adam,
the new "mother of all living," the "pure bride to her one
husband" (2 Co 11:2). It is "the Church of the living God,
the pillar and bulwark of the truth" (1 Tm 3:15). The continuity and identity of the Church in space and time in its
doctrinal, spiritual and sacramental being is guaranteed by
the Holy Spirit in the continuity and identity of the episcopate
within the community of the faithful.[21] The sacrament of the
ordained priesthood in the Church is the *mysterion* of the
objective presence of Christ in, with and for the body of
believers—his mystical bride, with whom he is "one spirit"
and "one flesh" always, "until the close of the ages" (Mt
28:20). The sacrament of the ordained priesthood guarantees
Christ's presence in the Church in all the fulness of his
messianic power, with all the fulness of grace and truth of
the eternal life of the kingdom of God which he brings to
mankind (cf Jn 1:1-18).

There are those who deny this doctrine of the catholic
tradition of the Church. Some say that the Church is an
institution established by God with seven sacraments, defined
as visible signs conferring invisible grace, and one of which
is the sacrament of "holy orders"—understood as being the

[21]See J. Zizioulas, "Apostolic Continuity and Orthodox Theology: Towards
a Synthesis of Two Perspectives," *St. Vladimir's Theological Quarterly* 19:2
(1975) 75-108.

exercise of a certain spiritual power and authority by selected members of the Church so that these members, chosen and consecrated as individuals, could represent Christ in the Church as his vicars and delegates. This view stresses the priestly vocation as one vocation among many, and emphasizes clerical powers and authority, prerogatives and privileges, and, of course, duties and ministries that do not belong to the members of the body, who have other vocations and ministries. For example, the priest has the power to celebrate the eucharist, to preach, to teach, to forgive sins, etc., which others do not have. It is in this sense that he is said to have a "priestly" vocation.

Others deny such a view of the priesthood and say that the Church is indeed an institution established by God with sacraments defined as visible signs conferring invisible grace, but that the ordained ministry of the Church is not one of these sacraments, which are only two in number: baptism and the Lord's Supper. Those who hold this view generally consider Christian faith as a matter of the faith of individuals, saved by grace through their personal acceptance of Jesus as Lord and Savior, with the priesthood of Christ operating invisibly in the Christian community through the "priesthood of all believers." Thus, in a word, there is no sacramental sign and guarantee of Christ's objective presence in the Church through an ordained priesthood, whose continuity, solidarity and identity in the faith and life of the Church with all the faithful guarantees the continuity, solidarity and identity of the faith and life of the Church itself. It is rather the case that the ordained ministers of the church communities exercise professional leadership roles, primarily through preaching, teaching, counseling and community administration.

Both of these views, according to the orthodox tradition of Christian faith, are incorrect.[22] They are incorrect because

[22]The "westernized dogmatics" of some modern Orthodox theologians tend to see the sacrament of priesthood along the lines of the first view presented, as generally the sacramental theology of modern Orthodox dogmatics following Latin scholastic patterns. See A. Schmemann, *Introduction to Liturgical Theology* (London: Faith Press, 1966), chapter 1, pp. 9-27. See also Schmemann, "Russian Theology: 1920-1972, An Introductory Survey,"

they express a wrong understanding of the Church and the sacraments. The Church, to put it simply and perhaps to risk grave misunderstanding, should not be understood as an institution possessing sacraments, which are defined as special, divinely instituted acts that yield special spiritual graces, however many there may be and however their operation is explained.[23] Rather, the Church herself is a sacrament, indeed *the sacrament par excellence,* having an essentially sacramental structure as her official, "institutional" expression and life.

The Church is the "great mystery" of man's communion with God through Christ and the Spirit. It is the mystery of new life in the new humanity of the new Adam in the new creation. The Church is the new Eve, the new "mother of all living," the "pure bride to her one husband"—Christ. As such, the Church is *one* with the unity of God and his Son and Holy Spirit; *holy* with his holiness; *catholic* with his fulness of divine being and life; *apostolic* with his divinely revealed doctrine and mission of salvation. As the "real presence" of the kingdom of God in this world, the Church has temporal institutions, organizations and offices, which are actualized differently in various historical, social and cultural settings and forms. But as an essentially sacramental reality, the Church cannot be reduced to or wholly identified with any of her purely historical expressions. Her essential being is rather the "mystery hidden for ages . . . but now made manifest in the saints" (Col 1:26), the mystery of human life becoming divine through communion with God. This life, "for us men and for our salvation," is given in the sacramental life of the Church, proclaimed in her inspired scriptures, defended in her dogmatic definitions, protected in her canonical norms, and witnessed in her deified members, the saints.

The ordained priesthood in and for the Church—and not

and C. Yannaras, "Theology in Present-Day Greece," *St. Vladimir's Theological Quarterly* 16:4 (1972) 172-214.

[23]The practice of numbering the sacraments and treating them in isolation from one another and from the whole life and experience of the Church is one of the "westernized" elements in contemporary theology that must be overcome.

over and apart from it—is, as we have said, the sacrament of
the presence of Christ himself in and for his body and his
bride. The priesthood of Christ is the priesthood of the
body. There are not two priesthoods, only one. When people
ask whether the ordained priest, bishop or presbyter "represents Christ" or "represents the faithful," the question is
unanswerable. When they place in opposition the "ordained
priesthood" and "all the believers," the opposition is unjustifiable and unreal. In the first place, the ordained priest does
not "represent" anyone, neither Christ nor the people. He is
not a vicar, delegate or "stand in" for anyone, neither for
the Lord nor for his body. Christ is in and with his body and
bride, as his body and bride are in and with him in the
gracious communion of one being and life guaranteed by the
Holy Spirit. In the "great mystery" of Christ and the Church,
the life of the head is the life of the body, and the priesthood
of the head is the priesthood of the members. As Christ himself is not the "vicarious delegate" of God to man and man
to God, but rather the fulness of divinity in human form and
the fulness of humanity in his divine person—in the presence
and presentation of God in and to man and, as such, the
presence and presentation of man in and to God—so the
ordained priest, in his sacramental being in the Church, is the
sacramental presence and presentation of Christ himself, in
and with his people: Christ as the one who "comes down from
heaven," and Christ as the one who is raised from the dead
and lives forever as high priest in the presence of God on
our behalf (cf Hebrews). As Christ is our high priest, pastor,
teacher and bishop because he *first* is the presence and presentation of God in our midst, and as Christ takes us to the
Father because he *first* brings the Father to us, so the ordained
priest in the Church is the sacramental head of the community
because he *first* is the sacramental image of Christ in the
community as coming from God. This is the critical point that
centers the official, sacramental gathering of the Christian
community in and around its bishop and priest, rather than—
speaking in human terms—placing the bishop and priest in
the context of the gathering. This point was made, I believe,
already in the second century, when it was written: "Where

the bishop appears, *there* let the people be, just as where Jesus Christ is, *there* is the Catholic Church."[24] The ordained priest "presents" Christ's body and bride to the Father because he first "presents" Christ to his body and bride.

As a sacrament of the Church, the ordained priesthood is not an individual vocation or a personal charism or gift. It is not one of the several ministries of the members of the church community. It is rather the sacramental manifestation of the ministry of Christ in and for the Church, in which all of the personal and partial ministries of the members are rooted, fulfilled, validated and evaluated. In this sense it can be said that the ordained priest in the Church, like Jesus himself, has no particular vocation. He has none *as priest,* i.e., in his sacramental being and office, because *as priest,* he is the sacramental term of reference, norm of evaluation and source of fulfilment of all churchly and human ministries. In the opposite way, it can be said that the ordained priest, in his sacramental character *as priest,* has all vocations, precisely because *sacramentally*—like Christ himself—he has none.

The ordained priest is the one who, in his sacramental being as the "presentation" of Christ in and for the Church, is the "presentation" of the image of "the way, the truth and the life" of all particular and personal human activities and ministries—including even his own as one member of the body, both in his personal life and in the existential actual-ization and personal exercise of his sacramental office (which, in fact, can hardly be separated). The pastoral office of the ordained priest witnesses to the pastoral dimensions of all human vocations. His priestly character testifies to the fact that all human being and life must be offered to God. His teaching ministry is the measure and norm of all human teaching. His service of judgment and discernment—"rightly defining the word of truth"—provides the pattern for all who execute justice. His healing ministry demonstrates what genuine healing is, as his office of reconciliation and forgive-ness bears testimony to this abiding factor in the whole of human life. Finally, his position as "servant," with absolutely no purely temporal and secular interests, is the sign that

[24]Ignatius of Antioch, *To the Smyrneans* 8:2; see also Zizioulas.

everything that belongs to "this world" is either fulfilled in God's kingdom or forever perishes and passes away.

With such an objective sacramental vocation, the "qualifications" for being a priest in Christ's Church are not reducible to any particular human talents or skills, and the "job description" for the sacramental office defies any neat outline. The priest must know the apostolic scriptures and the orthodox doctrines, but he need not be an academic theologian or scholar. He must teach, but he need not be a pedagogue. He must preach, but rhetorical eloquence is no necessity. He must shepherd the flock, but "pastoral counseling" may be someone else's "specialty." He must administer, but purely organizational and executive skills may belong to another. He must pray, of course, but the "life of prayer" as a particular charism is not a requirement.

The qualifications that the holder of the episcopal and presbyteral offices in the Church must have are traditionally more "external" and "objective" than they are "internal" and "subjective." His specific charisms, talents and skills may vary, but his objective image must be vivid and firm. He must be a male member of the church community, fully identified with the faith of the Church and professing it soundly and clearly while striving to fulfil it in his own personal life. He must be physically whole, the husband of one wife or a professed celibate. If he is married, his wife and children must be members of the Church (at least those children living in his household and under his domestic care). He must have no record of grave sin after baptism, specifically including the shedding of blood, sexual immorality and public scandal, and he must be of "good reputation" before those outside the Church as well as within. He must not be involved in political, economic or military affairs, or in any secular business, and neither can his wife. His personal "lifestyle" must be such that it does not conflict with his sacramental being and office. Thus, for example, should he feel called to some specific form of social or political activity, to government service, to monastic contemplation or to legal advocacy; or should he feel obliged to enter the military, or take a second wife or to propagate some specific form of Christian "action" or "piety" as an all-consuming "prophetic" activity: he should give up his sacramental office. Being an ordained priest, he may work at an acceptable job if necessary, for the purpose of sustaining his life and that of his dependents, but he should not have any particular work as his primary "vocation" while being a priest "on the side." The priest should be wholly dedicated to his priesthood, which he understands not as a "profession" or "job," but which he freely accepts as a sacramental office of the Church, an element of the Church's very being and life.[25]

The priest, in his sacramental being, is not the bearer of specific gifts, or the most gifts, or the best gifts. He is not the "holiest member of the Church," or the one who "takes the faith most seriously." He does not have any particular moral or ethical standard of behavior different from that of anyone else who is baptized in Christ, sealed with the Holy Spirit and participating in the eucharistic offering. He is certainly not someone who has a special "religious vocation." Every human being has a "religious vocation," simply by being created in the image and likeness of God and being saved by the incarnation of Christ and the descent of the Holy Spirit, as an Adam or an Eve within the human and church community. There is little doubt that any given person is more talented or

[25]See the canons of Nicea 1, 2, 9, 10, 17; Ancyra 2, 14; Neocaesarea 1, 8, 9; Antioch 2, 5, 13, 17, 18, 21, 22; Laodicea 3, 4, 13, 24, 36, 55, 58; Chalcedon 3, 6, 7, 10, 13; *In Trullo* 3, 4, 9, 10, 13, 20, 22, 23, 24, 27, 31, 70; African Code 21, 35, 36, 40, 54; 2 Nicea 2, 4, 5, 10, 15, 16; Apostolic Canons 5, 6, 15, 17, 18, 23, 25, 27, 29, 30, 36, 42, 44, 51, 54, 55, 57, 58, 59, 61, 65, 67, 77, 78. The question of "part-time priests" (like "auxiliary bishops") without a specific pastoral office is problematic. Such positions can be justified only on the basis of pastoral *oikonomia*, with the condition that each church community has one "archpastor," be he the archbishop of a diocese or the archpresbyter of a parish, with those under his pastoral guidance and direction performing certain duties of assistance for the welfare of the community, in which instances (e.g., celebrating and distributing the eucharist, anointing the sick, burying the dead), the "part-time priest" still functions sacramentally *in persona Christi*, and not as the "vicar" or "delegate" of any other person holding sacramental office in the Church. A bishop or presbyter in the Church never "represents" another; he is always the sacramental presentation of Christ himself. While on the presbyteral level the "part-time priest" may be understood and accepted rather easily, I personally believe that "vicar" or "auxiliary" bishops can hardly be justified according to traditional orthodox ecclesiology.

skilled in one way or another than is the bishop or presbyter of his church community; and there is hardly a doubt that any number of the members of the Church are personally "more holy" than those who hold the pastoral office—a point, in any case, impossible to prove and, given normal and healthy Christian conditions, wholly outside anyone's spiritual interest and concern.

All human beings, and certainly all members of the Church, are "called to be saints" (Rm 1:7). All are called to die and rise with Christ, and to "put on Christ" (Ga 3:27). All are called to be "temples of the Holy Spirit" (1 Co 6:19, 3:16-17) and "partakers of the divine nature" (2 Pt 1:4). But not all are created and called to do so in the same way. Humanity, like divinity, is a "community." There are different modes of being and different ways of living in which the various members of the community are to live and to act, so that, in harmony and unity, in mutual fulfilment and support, the Church might be the realization of "saved humanity," truly expressing and reflecting the trinitarian being and life of God, with one common will and operation, one common mind and spirit, and—as it is said of the Jerusalem Church in book of Acts—"one heart and soul" (Ac 4:32).

The female members of the church community are excluded from holding the sacramental office of bishop and presbyter in the Church not because they are "inferior" in their humanity to the male members of the Church, or less holy, talented or skilled. Indeed, if we use the word "exclude" in its common, popular sense, then to speak of women being "excluded" from the sacramental ministry is an impossible way of stating the issue in the first place, for it supposes that women can hold the office but may not do so for some debilitating reason. To put it this way is like saying that the Holy Spirit is "excluded" from being the Logos and the Christ, the high priest, head and husband of the Church, because of some defect or weakness in the Spirit's divinity. This, of course, is nonsense. And it is just as nonsensical to speak of women being "excluded" from the priestly office of the Church.

In the same way, to claim that the fact that women are not ordained to the episcopal and presbyteral offices of the

Church is discriminatory, demeaning and degrading, demonstrating the false and unjust view of feminine "inequality" with males, is also nonsensical. Once more, it is like saying that the Holy Spirit is discriminated against, degraded and demeaned by not being the Logos and Son of God. In fact, it is a dogma of the orthodox, catholic Church that the Holy Spirit is absolutely equal to the Son of God, and to the Father himself, personally and substantially, and is in no way "unequal" or "inferior." Within the Godhead—if not within fallen humanity—to be fully and absolutely equal does not mean to possess interchangeable forms of being and to perform interchangeable actions and ministries.

As there is a *taxis* in the divine Trinity according to traditional, orthodox theology—an *order,* and one might even say a *hierarchy,* if one does not interpret this as some sort of ontological and essential "subordinationism"—so there is a *taxis* in humanity, an *order* and *hierarchy.*[26] This must be so, for the very perfection and fulness of being and life, both human and divine. *Order,* and even *hierarchy,* do not annihilate "equality." Catholic Christian dogma speaks of the "second" and "third" persons of the Holy Trinity, and calls them "consubstantial, coequal, coenthroned and coreigning" in perfect divine unity and communion.[27] This vision of reality is "illogical" to those who reason according to the logic of "this world" and who consider man's existence between bodily

[26]Orthodox Vespers of Pentecost.

[27]For many people, any implication of "order" or "hierarchy" in the Trinity is considered to be heretical because it suggests essential and personal inequality. This is, I believe, the result of a doctrine of the trinitarian God not scripturally and sacramentally based, but rooted in a view of reality that has its source outside the Christian experience—a view that denies any genuine hypostatic and personal distinction and differentiation in the Godhead and considers the three trinitarian names as modalistic expressions of a unipersonal (or suprapersonal or impersonal) God; or as mere "relations," however "subsistent" or "interpersonal"; or as symbols created about the deity arising out of human experience, which can be changed and altered according to cultural patterns. It is the inability to accept the three divine persons as revealed in the scriptures, prayed to through and in the liturgy, and known and experienced in the spiritual life of the Church, which makes "hierarchy" and "equality" mutually exclusive and contradictory for many, both in relation to God and man. See Jewett, 43-5, 69-71, 85, 133, *et passim.* Indeed, these terms, and their realization, are illogical and contradictory if one's logic is not a logic "proper to God," the traditional λόγος θεοπρεπής.

birth (if not conception) and physical death to be the sum and substance of human life. But according to the logic "proper to divinity," which understands human life to be in the image of God, it is clear and convincing, and its basis is spiritual experience.

> For the Spirit searches everything, even the depths of God . . . so also no one comprehends the thoughts of God except the Spirit of God. Now we have received not the spirit of the world, but the Spirit which is from God, that we might understand the gifts bestowed upon us by God. And we impart this in words not taught by human wisdom but taught by the Spirit, interpreting spiritual truths to those who possess the Spirit. The unspiritual man does not receive the gifts of the Spirit of God, for they are folly to him, and he is not able to understand them because they are spiritually discerned . . . "For who has known the mind of the Lord so as to instruct him?" [Is 40:13] But we have the mind of Christ. (1 Co 2:10-16)

Conclusion

It is the thesis of this paper that there exists a uniquely feminine manner of human being and life which has as many forms of realization as there are women created by God. It is the assertion as well that feminine humanity is absolutely necessary for the perfection and fulness of human life, and without it the human community cannot reflect the being and life of God, the uncreated Trinity. Thirdly, it is the position that it is not weakness, inferiority or sin that prevents women from holding the episcopal and presbyteral sacramental offices of the Christian Church, but rather their unique mode of human being and action, which is incompatible with exercising these positions in the community. Fourthly, it is my conviction that to speak of women as being "excluded" from the Christian priesthood is absurd and nonsensical, for "exclusion" supposes a possible "inclusion," which does not in fact exist.

It is my conviction as well that not only the "well-being" but the "very being" of the Church requires more than just a sacramental priesthood utilizing only certain male members of the body who fulfil the requirements: the "very being" of the Church also requires, in addition to and among the many individual members with their personal talents and gifts, the presence of feminine humanity, whose natural, divinely created mode of human being and action patterns and reflects, *within the order of creation,* the mode of being and action of the Holy Spirit of God within the Godhead and in the divine dispensation of the creation, salvation and deification of the world. Should women seek and succeed to be ordained to the episcopal and presbyteral offices of the Church, it would be, in my opinion, a violation of the orthodox, catholic tradition of faith and spiritual life, and must be opposed by those committed to this vision and practice of human life because it would violate human communality as created by God in his image and likeness, which is reflected in the sacramental structures and spiritual life of the Christian Church and its members. The fact that women can be found who desire the offices of the Church's sacramental priesthood, and who can read, speak, sing, wear vestments and hold the chalice, is no justification that they should be blessed to do so. The fact that they *can* is no proof that they *may* or *should.* There are sufficient examples in human expertise to show that there are many actions that humans can and have taken, but whose results have proven anything but fruitful and edifying for the life of the human community. The fact that within the life of this world there are actual distortions and abnormalities within the human community requiring certain "accommodations" and "compromises" for life to continue is no argument that these distortions and abnormalities should be introduced into the sacramental structures and spiritual life of the Christian Church. The fact that women are called upon—and sometimes are even glorified by the Church as saints—for leadership in the secular order is no argument that they should therefore be ordained to the sacramental offices of bishop and priest within the church community.

The Church, in the midst of all temptations and corruptions of human life brought about by the voluntary or involuntary loss of the vision of perfect human community revealed by God, has the mission to proclaim, propagate and preserve this vision for the sake of human salvation and life. Those faithful to the vision of life given in the Church, therefore, must continue at all costs and in all conditions to assert the fact that humans are created male and female in the image and likeness of God; that human sexual difference and interrelation are essential for human perfection and deification; that the image of this perfection is found in Christ and the Church; that heterosexual marriage of one husband and one wife for eternity, patterned after the relationship between Christ and the Church, is the ideal of life for human community in this world; that the monastic vocation is a divinely inspired charism for those who "can receive it" (Mt 19:19) in anticipation of life in the kingdom of God; and that the sacramental priesthood of the Christian Church, as the sacramental "presentation" in and for the Church of Christ himself—the last Adam, the head of his body, the Bridegroom of his bride and the unique high priest, teacher, pastor and bishop of his people—must be exercised only by those members of the Church who, by creation and calling, are able to do so, which means in actuality only certain male members of the Church.

When Christ comes in glory at the end of the age to establish God's kingdom through the "marriage of the Lamb" with "his bride [who] has made herself ready" by the Spirit who says "Come!" (cf Rv 19-22), there will be no Church, no sacraments, no priesthood, no mission, no theological disputation. God will be with his people, which is "prepared as a bride for her husband," and "he will wipe away every tear and death shall be no more . . . nor crying, nor pain anymore, for the former things have passed away" (Rv 21:1-4). Christ will submit all to the Father, "that God may be all, and in all" (1 Co 15:28). But until Christ comes, it is the task of God's people to bear witness to his teaching about human life within the life of his Church by the grace of his Spirit. To those who seek worldly wisdom, this view will be foolishness. For those who seek power, this way will be scandalous.

But for those who believe, it will always remain "the power and wisdom of God" (1 Co 1:24).

A REPLY TO CRITICISM

I am grateful to those, including our students at St. Vladimir's Seminary, who offered criticism of my essay on the male character of the Christian priesthood. My reply to this criticism is the following.

Theological Method

Criticism was made first of all of the method I used in writing the essay. Some said that I had obviously decided, before any theological analysis and reflection, that only certain male members of the Christian Church may be ordained to the episcopate and the priesthood according to Orthodox doctrine, and that my writing was merely an attempt to "prove" what I had already prejudicially predetermined. Some said as well that the article was anything but open-minded, objective and scientific. I would certainly agree that there is a point to this criticism, and yet I would also contend that it is not altogether accurate.

What I had hoped to do in the essay was to take as my starting point the absolutely indisputable fact that the Church —which has had women saints of all sorts, including women secular rulers, some of whom have been given the title "equal to the apostles"—nevertheless has never had women bishops and priests. I took this as a "given," as a matter of factual data. I then proceeded to ask the question: Are there sound theological reasons for this fact or not? In order to answer this question, I proceeded along lines I also consider to be objective and undisputed, at least for Orthodox theology: to analyze the question in the light of the official teachings of the Orthodox Church concerning the Holy Trinity and the

revelation of God in Christ and the Holy Spirit. I attempted
to do this by reflecting on what is given in the Bible and
church tradition, in the liturgy, the councils, the fathers, the
canons and the saints of the Church, all of which, for Orthodox theologians, are the undisputed sources for understanding
and explaining the teachings and practices of the Church. This
method, I contend, is not a "prejudiced" method—unless
acceptance of the scriptural, dogmatic and liturgical data of
the Church as the basis for theological reflection and understanding is considered as inadmissible prejudgment and pre-
determination. No Orthodox theologian, I should think, can
be thus minded and still be Orthodox. And no man of good
will, I should like to hope, would consider such a method as
unscientific, if being "scientific" means to observe, analyze
and explain a given reality as it reveals itself to the observer
in its own context and on its own terms. One may reject certain
data as irrelevant to the question under consideration. But if
one accepts the "givens" in any discussion as the proper
"givens" for analysis and explanation, then the only proper
and "scientific" thing to do is to take them as they are given
and to work with them. This is what I attempted to do in
my article.

The Apophatic Character of Theology

Another criticism of my position was that I violated the
essentially apophatic character of Orthodox Christian theology.
The point was made that according to the church fathers
and Orthodox theology in general, the essence of God is
unknown and unknowable by creatures, and all human words,
concepts, images and symbols about God are just that: human
words and concepts which strictly speaking cannot be applied
to God. They are rather the confession and expression of
limited human experiences of the divine and are psychologically, socially, subjectively and culturally determined. The contention at this point was that in different times and places
men speak differently about God, and that in our own time
and place the words and symbols about the essentially ineffa-

ble and inconceivable God are not those of the past, even the
past of the Bible and the fathers. Therefore, the affirmation
of the fatherhood of God and the sonship of the Logos, along
with the traditional affirmations about the being and activity
of the Holy Spirit in *theologia* and *oikonomia,* cannot be
employed as an absolute basis for understanding and explaining human being and life, especially sexual life, as I have
attempted to do in my essay. The critical point here is that
the very apophatic nature of Orthodox theology forbids me
to do what I have attempted to do.

Here I would only say that I shall never agree with anyone who says that apophatic theology means that all words,
concepts, images and symbols about God are merely human
expressions about a God who is so unknowable that ultimately
we know nothing and can say nothing about him. The Christian faith and the Christian experience are rooted in the fact
that God has revealed himself to his creatures, that he has
made himself known through Christ and the Holy Spirit in
the life of his covenanted people in a way that is as perfect
and full as the fallen conditions of this sinful world allow.
The unyielding affirmations of Christians about the trinitarian
character of God and about the incarnation of the Word in
human flesh are not a violation of the fundamentally apophatic
character of Orthodox Christian theology. Apophaticism in
theology is not the same as total ignorance. It is not the claim
that we know nothing whatsoever of God, in reference to
whom our human expressions are ultimately meaningless
and useless. It is rather a way—the traditional Orthodox
Christian way—of knowing God: of knowing and affirming
the fact that the God who reveals himself in creation and in
the dispensation of salvation in his Word and his Spirit is
ultimately beyond creaturely comprehension. It is the affirmation that divine reality is always infinitely more than and infinitely other than whatever can be known and claimed about
it. It is the affirmation that the inner being of the Father and
the Son and the Holy Spirit remains eternally and essentially
beyond what creatures can experience and know. It is the
affirmation that what can be known of God in Christ and the
Spirit in the Church is known by faith, by repentance, by

poverty of spirit and purity of heart in the "communion of love," which surpasses discursive reasoning and intellectual conceptualization. But it is not the denial of any knowledge whatsoever. It is certainly not the denial of the Holy Trinity: the transcendent lordship of the Father, the kenotic incarnation of the Son, and the sanctifying indwelling of the Holy Spirit in creatures made divine by grace.

In general, I believe that one of the main theological issues confronting Christians today is the proper understanding of the apophatic way in theology and spiritual life. All too often the apophatic way is wrongly understood to be the denial of any real knowledge of God at all, with the corresponding denial (often parading under the guise of self-deprecating humility) that our theological words and concepts have any meaning at all. Such a denial is in fact a denial of divine revelation and of theology itself. It is a denial of every word of the Bible and the liturgy and the testimony of every prophet, apostle and saint. It is certainly a denial of Jesus Christ. If there are indeed no "words adequate to God" —to the extent that any human expressions are adequate to divine reality—then we humans are left ignorantly wallowing in the subjectively created imaginations of our own invention. Such is not Orthodox Christianity or Orthodox theology; it is not the teaching of Christ and the Church.

Logos—Male; Spirit—Female

Another criticism of my position was that any intuition and reflection that leads to a comparison between the Logos and man and the Holy Spirit and woman is wrong: first of all because there is no sexuality in God; and also because the divine hypostases of the Word and the Spirit only indicate that there are *persons* of the Godhead, who come forth from the Father by "generation" and "procession" and who at best can be imagined in humanity by different *persons* and not different *sexes*. Here my own point is simply that there are, as a matter of fact, two "modes of divine existence" within the Trinity whose hypostatic characteristics and manner of

interrelating, especially as they are revealed in the divine
oikonomia of creation and salvation, bear a striking resemblance to the "mode of human existence" and manner of
interrelating created and commanded by God for men and
women in the Bible and the Church, in the Old and the New
Testaments. And, it might be noted, this intuition of mine
has been observed and affirmed by others as well: the church
fathers, the Christian liturgy, and several modern theological
and spiritual writers, such as Serge Verhovskoy, Fr. Alexander Schmemann, Vladimir Lossky, C.S. Lewis, Edith Stein
(Sister Benedicta à Cruce in the Carmelite Order) and Joan
Schaupp (in her book *Woman: Image of the Holy Spirit*).
There is of course no sexuality in God. But the Holy Trinity
is the divine archetype for human being and life. Man *is*
made in the image and according to the likeness of God, male
and female. In the created order and within the boundaries
of creaturely existence, the human *is* a reflection of the divine.
Human nature does mirror the divine nature. Something of
what the divine reality is, is manifested and realized in what
human beings are. The divine reality is a Trinity of divine
persons in a unity of divine nature, within which the one God
and Father, the *principium divinitatis,* is manifested eternally
in two forms of divine being and personhood—namely, that
of the Word and the Spirit—while human nature images the
nature of the same one God and Father in two forms of
human existence—namely, that of male and female, albeit in
a multitude of created human persons. The fact that there is
but one Logos and one Holy Spirit, yet many men and many
women, is a fact to be dealt with. But it is a fact which, in
my opinion, is irrelevant to the fundamental intuition that
there is something to be made of the comparison between the
Logos and the Spirit in eternity and in the economy of creation and salvation, and man and woman in the created order.
I continue to believe that a comparison between what we
know about divine reality and what we know about the
human is proper in theological and spiritual reflection and
analysis.

The point was also made that all humans are logical and
spiritual; that each human being, male or female, is made in

the image of God; that Christ is not simply the perfect male, but the perfect human and the image of perfection for all human beings, male and female; and that the Virgin Mary, as the image of the saved who hear the Word of God and keep it by the power of the Holy Spirit, is the image of the perfect response to God for all humans, both male and female, and not just for woman. All this was noted in apparent opposition to my comparison between Christ and men and the Spirit and women. On this point I would only say that proper distinctions must be made. It is certainly true that all humans are made in God's image and likeness, and that the Son of God has become human in the incarnation as the pattern for perfection for all humans, which perfection is perfectly realized by creatures in the Virgin Mary. It is undoubtedly true that Christ's humanity, like that of the Virgin Mother, is the humanity of everyone, both men and women. But it is equally true and hardly to be denied—unless we deny both the Bible and church tradition—that there is a sense in which Jesus, as the bridegroom, head and husband, is a pattern for males; while the Church, imaged in the Virgin Mary, is a pattern for females, as the bride, the body and the wife. In short, there is a sense in which both Christ and Mary exemplify the perfection of human nature, a sense in which Mary is the perfect disciple and imitator of Christ. But there is also a sense in which Christ and Mary exemplify in their persons the perfection of the dual forms of human being and behavior: male and female. It might be said that in revealing human perfection—commanded as possible and necessary for all human beings—to the world, Jesus does so in a particularly male fashion; while in her revelation as the perfect human by grace, the Virgin Mary demonstrates in a particularly feminine form what all human beings must be like.

In reference to the issue of the sacramental priesthood and the Church as the body of the faithful, the comparison follows: Christ is the high priest who reveals the priestly character of all of human life, both male and female; while Mary, as the "image of the Church," reveals the sacrificed and sanctified character of the whole of humanity as it has been offered to the Father through the Son. And yet Christ, in the uniqueness of his incarnate person as the high priest, head and husband of his body and his bride, is imaged in the sacramental priesthood precisely in male form; while Mary remains forever for Christians as the unique person who stands as the icon of the Church, the bride and the body of the incarnate Logos, offered to the Father and brought into his presence at the marriage feast of the Lamb in an explicitly feminine way.

I see as wholly consistent and harmonious the comparison between the Logos and the Spirit, Yahweh and Israel, Christ and the Church as imaged in the person of the Spirit-filled Virgin, the sacramental priest and the body of the faithful, the bridegroom and the bride, the husband and the wife, man and woman, Adam and Eve. These comparisons run through the Bible and the liturgy and are reflected in the theological, spiritual and moral doctrines and practices of the Christian Church. I would also continue to defend the position that these images are given by God; that they reveal fundamental and critical truths about God and man; that they cannot be changed or violated in any way; and that they must be examined, understood and explained if we are to be saved and come to the knowledge of the truth. It may well be, however, that the "explanation" of this vision will serve only to distort the reality itself. I am beginning to think so myself, especially as the debate about human sexuality and the sacramental priesthood goes on. But in our fallen world of contention and debate, such "explanation"—understood for what it is, namely, a dissection and distortion of reality—appears to be unavoidable and inevitable.

A Spiritual Vision and Experience

This leads to my final comment. A bishop of the Church, whom I greatly respect, told me that he considered all "explanations" made thus far of the male character of the Christian priesthood to be unconvincing and inadequate, including my own. He told me confidentially and, I believe, with great charity that he found my essay to be more an exercise in "fantasy" and "imagination" than in theology as such. This was obviously not easy for me to take, and when I, clearly looking for some consolation, shared the story with a friend, I was told that I should not take it so hard. My friend reminded me that the Song of Songs and the book of Revelation also are more like "fantasy" and "imagination" than like much of what passes for theology, not to mention the liturgy of the Church and many mystical writings of the saints. My discomfort remains, however, for my essay was intended to be theology. But perhaps there still is a comforting point, one which I tried to make in one of the footnotes in the original article. That is that the issues of human sexuality and the sacramental priesthood are, for Orthodox Christians, issues which belong to the inner life of the Church, issues in the area of what is traditionally called *dogma* rather than *kerygmata*. This means that their understanding and explanation, if such explanation there can be, will be available and meaningful only to those who have accepted Jesus Christ as Lord and Savior and have entered into the life of the Church through faith, repentance, purification and prayer, having eyes willing to see, ears willing to hear and a mind willing to understand. In any case, the proper explanation, if such there be, will most certainly never be the result of "disputing about words, which does no good, but only ruins the hearers" (2 Tm 2:14).

The Spirit of the Female Priesthood

By Deborah Belonick*

A Theological Revolution

After the publication of her classic work on feminism, *The Feminine Mystique,*[1] in the early 1960s, Betty Friedan was asked what she thought would be the most radical change caused by the women's movement. "I can't tell you now," she answered. "You wouldn't believe it anyhow . . . it is theological."[2] That statement came from a woman who, although not considering herself particularly religious, knew that by and by the women's movement would cause a psychological and, eventually, a spiritual, religious revolution. A new way of looking at God and humanity, a new theology, would be created.

Friedan's prediction has come to pass. Many books by theologians with a feminist point of view are being published, and new liturgical rites composed by women are being popularized in some Christian and Jewish congregations. Some

*Deborah Belonick is a recent graduate of St. Vladimir's Seminary. Married and the mother of two sons, she serves on the Faith and Order Commission of the NCC. A revised version of her graduation thesis has been published under the title *Feminism in Christianity: An Orthodox Christian Response.* The present article is copyrighted © 1981 by Deborah Belonick and is reprinted with permission.

[1]Betty Friedan, *The Feminine Mystique* (New York: W. W. Norton, 1963). This is the work that prompted the women's movement in the twentieth century.

[2]Betty Friedan, *It Changed my Life* (New York: Random House, 1963) 290.

135

women have begun investigating mythological literature and advocate a return to worship of the "Mother Goddess" instead of "our Father in heaven." Many denominations are changing portions of the language in hymns and educational materials to reflect an inclusion of the female sex. In short, many theologians who consider themselves to be both Christian and feminist have begun adjusting mainstream Christian thought—adding a "woman's touch" some would say—in order to wrest Christianity from what they feel for centuries has been a patriarchal prison.

Perhaps the most noticeable verification of the effects of the women's movement on the realm of religion is the expanding presence of the female priesthood, and the movement toward it, in traditional Christian communities. Many Christians of various denominations have heralded the advent of the ordination of women as an action of the Holy Spirit, an indication that the Spirit of God is working to liberate the Christian communities from a sexist and oppressive patriarchal structure, which by its very nature sustains divisive, sexist attitudes between women and men.[3] The female priesthood has been looked upon by proponents as a healthy sign that Christian churches have spiritually and culturally evolved to the point where they can "admit" women to the clergy instead of regarding them as "second-class" Christians, and at last the churches are being true to the words of St. Paul: "There is neither Jew nor Greek, there is neither slave nor free, there is neither male nor female, for you are all one in Christ Jesus" (Ga 3:28). Just as injustice toward women has been eroding in the surrounding culture, so too is it eroding in traditional Christian structures. And when the culturally determined stereotypes of women and men are removed from the Christian community, it finally will become the place where all can share in the freedom, equality and justice that Jesus Christ had promised.

All Christian communities, including the Orthodox Christian Church, are bound by Jesus Christ to answer these

[3]Such an attitude was prevalent at a World Council of Churches consultation of September 1979 in Klingenthal, France, on "The Ordination of Women in Ecumenical Perspective," which this author attended.

feminist convictions, since they have been admonished by the apostle John: "Beloved, do not believe every spirit, but test the spirits to see whether they are of God; for many false prophets have gone out into the world" (1 Jn 4:1). At this point in history, Christian communities must affirm or deny whether the female priesthood is the fruit of the action of the Holy Spirit, which must not be resisted.

Upon close investigation of the theology that underlies, sustains and produces the symbol of the female priest, we find that we are faced with a theological revolution, not an evolution. The theology that buttresses the female priesthood is at times little more than philosophy extracted from the women's movement, which was adopted and accepted by some as "theology" to support the ordination of women. Moreover, this underlying "feminist theology" cannot be identified as being within the Judeo-Christian tradition, understood as the tradition of the people who have their roots in the Bible and the councils of the Church. This feminist theology is in fact so opposed to the Bible and tradition of the Christian Church that one may say that two different worldviews, two visions of God and humanity, are present. And since there is such a wide divergence between the two theological systems, only *one* can claim to be truly in the Spirit of Jesus Christ; the two viewpoints are too distinct for both to be called "Christian."[4] One is forced to speak either in the category of "feminist-liberationist priesthood" or of "male-Christian priesthood," when given the fact that the female priesthood is based on a theology in opposition to traditional doctrines of the Church and the creative and salvific acts of God.

Accordingly, admitting women to the priesthood should not be the main issue of debate. The question of women's ordination should not be an endless quarrel about whether women are "good enough," "clean enough" or "smart enough" to wear vestments, carry chalices, marry, baptize, counsel, preach or theologize as well as men. To be sure, women *are*. The question is much deeper than that. The point is that the theological arguments supporting the ordination

[4]This conclusion follows from Ephesians 4:4-5: "There is one body and one Spirit . . . one Lord, one faith, one baptism."

of women ultimately are opposed to the Christian faith and its teachings about salvation. Furthermore, it can be illustrated that this theology shares a secular feminist philosophy, strengthened by the women's movement. In other words, a secular ideology, and not the Holy Spirit, is the fuel for the theology behind the female priesthood, and this has caused basic distortions in traditional Christian doctrine.[5]

The concept of female priesthood is the tip of a great iceberg of theological misconceptions underlying it; it is primarily a *theological* rather than a social, psychological or political issue. Our purpose, therefore, is not to discuss the symbol of the female priest, but to investigate those theological doctrines necessarily undergirding it. These doctrines include perceptions of Jesus Christ, the bodily resurrection, human sexuality and the persons of the Holy Trinity that are contrary to Orthodox Christian tradition and to basic Christian doctrines. By studying these feminist doctrines, one can discover the theological errors accompanying the symbol of the female priest.

The Feminist Vision of Jesus Christ

Jesus Christ, the central figure of the Christian faith, was a male, and that fact is sometimes disconcerting to a number of feminist Christians. It is especially disconcerting when one considers the office of the sacramental priesthood.

The traditional argument for the male priesthood is that Jesus Christ was a male and that he selected only male apostles to continue the presence of his unique high priesthood in the community. More specifically, within the Orthodox

[5]Many feminists would contend that the original push for the female priesthood came from within the Christian communities, and not from the women's movement. The facts, however, seem otherwise. Elizabeth Carroll, R.S.M., claims that the decisions of Vatican II on the dignity of persons plus "the whole cultural movement towards a fairer evaluation of women awakened Catholic women to their potentials." See her "Women in Ministry," in *Woman: New Dimensions,* ed. Walter J. Burghardt, S.J. (New York: Paulist Press, 1975) 84, n.4. Elizabeth Schussler Fiorenza, in the same volume, speaks of transforming Christian theology from a feminist perspective ("Feminist Theology as a Critical Theology of Liberation," 35).

Christian tradition, the priest is the one who bears the relationship of "father" to the rest of the congregation. He is the presence of Jesus Christ, who bore a "masculine" mode toward the Church: as Husband, Head, Bridegroom, Servant and Lord. The priest is ordained to bear the presence of the priesthood, headship and relationship of Jesus Christ to the community, until the Lord comes again. The Orthodox Church believes that such a relationship can be borne only by a male, and therefore only males are ordained to the priesthood.

Feminized-Christians[6] have attacked this traditional argument in several ways, most commonly by insisting that the sex of Jesus Christ cannot be given import when discussing the office of the priesthood. To do so would be a theological error. First, they say, the fact that Jesus was anatomically male is a superfluous fact, as significant as his having had brown eyes or having been a Jew; it is a fact that should be overlooked when deciding who should be admitted to the priesthood. One's sex, say feminists, is just a physical description, and since the priest does not have to physically resemble Jesus Christ in any other way, women should not be barred from the priesthood on that basis.

Second, claim feminized-Christians, though Jesus Christ was biologically male, psychologically he was both masculine and feminine. He fit no "machismo" role, but combined within himself the best of all human traits; he was both strong and compassionate, both authoritative and meek. He was simply human, a person—the image of the perfect "whole" human being, the perfect "androgyne," as some feminists would state.[7] In addition, since he took on human nature common to women and men, and saved both, why then should women not be included in the priesthood? Indeed, it would be a sin *not* to include them, since Jesus Christ saved the human race, and not just males! Feminist theologians emphasize the importance of the humanity of Jesus Christ

[6]"Feminized-Christians" will be the term used in this article to designate those believers who have embraced feminist philosophy as a directive of their Christian faith.

[7]Ruth Tiffany Barnhouse, M.D., "An Examination of the Ordination of Women to the Priesthood in Terms of the Symbolism of the Eucharist," in *Women and Orders,* ed. Robert J. Heyer (New York: Paulist Press, 1974) 23.

and deemphasize the importance of his male sexuality. Dr. Sonya Quitslund put it succinctly: "we have to ask, 'Was Christ, as God, taking on humanness, or was He exclusively taking on maleness when He came to earth?' It seems to me that if it was only maleness, then He couldn't redeem the whole human race, and I don't believe the church would want to dispute that."[8]

Third, contend feminists, the male body of Jesus Christ was only a temporary vehicle, useful in spreading the gospel message. (If Jesus had been incarnate as a female, claims one feminist, his message would have been disregarded in the first century.)[9] After the resurrection, these feminists say, his body was destroyed. The resurrected Christ represents the whole of humanity; neither female nor male anatomically, the resurrected Christ is a glorified spirit. Thus, feminist theologians deny the bodily resurrection of Jesus Christ in order to present an image of the risen Lord as a sort of "spirit of humanity" freed from the entrapment of an eternally male body. The following statements express all of these sentiments: "As a living human being Christ was a man. His sex was part of him: yet it was not his wholeness, and when he died he was free from its limitations . . . The human Christ was the representative of the whole of humanity, and yet, women and men who are alive now must still accept the limitations of their bodies."[10] "It was necessary to pick a particular sex in which to incarnate . . . Jesus in the first century *had* to be and therefore was male, even though the living Christ was androgynous."[11]

It is clear that feminist theologians are intent on eroding the male image of Jesus Christ in order to theologically clear the path for a female priesthood. They have formulated several christological doctrines in their favor. However, their christology is not in keeping with Christian tradition. Indeed, their christology is quite opposed to Christian thought.

[8]Sonya Quitslund, quoted in Paul Wilkes, "Equal Rights on the Altar of God?" *The New York Times Magazine* (November 30, 1980) 106-8.

[9]Barnhouse, 23.

[10]Una Kroll, *Flesh of my Flesh* (London: Darton, Longman and Todd, 1975) 102-3.

[11]Barnhouse, 23.

Traditional Christology

No Orthodox theologian would deny that Jesus Christ took on a human nature common to both women and men. This doctrine has been expressed several times at several councils, and here the agreement with feminist theologians is complete: "Leontius of Jerusalem insists that Christ's hypostasis, since it is that of the Logos, is not 'particular' (εἰδικὴ) but 'common' (κοινή), and that this is the reason why Scripture designates Christ's manhood as being simply flesh; for Christ unites 'all of humanity' (πᾶσαν τὴν ἀνθρωπότητα), and not only one individual of the human race to the divinity. The term 'flesh' is a generic term designating human nature as a whole."[12] The Lord saved all of humanity by taking on human nature.

Indeed, theologians of the past often were consumed with proclaiming the common humanity of Jesus Christ, because it was an issue of their time. These theologians were dealing with heresies that taught that Jesus was superhuman, subhuman or "merely" human.[13] It was their task, therefore, to declare that Jesus Christ was truly consubstantial to women and men in their humanity, and to God in his divinity. The sexuality of Jesus Christ was considered, but hardly emphasized, since it was not an issue of consequence in the early centuries of the Church and no one challenged the masculinity of Jesus Christ.[14]

However, now that this doctrine of Christ's common humanity has been expressed by the Church, new questions about humanity itself have been raised in this era. It is the duty of the Church to try to explain this humanity and deal with questions not presented to the early Church—those on

[12]John Meyendorff, *Christ in Eastern Christian Thought* (Crestwood, N.Y.: SVS Press, 1975) 74. See also the letter of St. Cyril of Alexandria to John of Antioch; cf the *oros* of the Fourth Ecumenical Council (Chalcedon, 451).
[13]For an explanation of these debates, see Meyendorff, esp. 3-67.
[14]St. Gregory of Nazianzus, *Second Oration on Easter*. See also Theodore the Studite, quoted in Meyendorff, 186: "An indescribable Christ would also be an incorporal Christ; but Isaiah (8:3) describes him as a male being [ἄρρην τεχθείς]."

sexuality, femininity and masculinity, and the sexuality of Jesus Christ in particular—defining the lines between heresy and Orthodoxy. In regard to the sexuality[15] of Jesus Christ, then, one must search the Scriptures and the patristic writings for clues to traditional thought on this subject.

Feminists often ignore biblical imagery of Christ, which depicts the Lord as authoritative (Lk 20:1-8), as Bridegroom (Mt 9:14-15, Jn 3:28-30), as Head (Eph 5:23), as King (Lk 19:38), the slain Lamb (Rv 5:12), as Judge (Rv 19:11), as perfect Servant of the Church (Lk 22:27), as Son (Jn 1:18) and as Savior (Eph 5:21-32)—all typically masculine relationships. (He was not body, bride, handmaid or daughter.) They instead focus on the relatively few passages in regard to the motherly tenderness of the Lord (Lk 13:34).

In the Orthodox tradition, as the fourth-century theologian Gregory of Nazianzus notes, the functions and actions of Jesus Christ are seen as overwhelmingly heroic, courageous, sacrificial and authoritative. Certainly, humility, mercy, compassion and love were among the qualities of Jesus, but, according to Gregory, these qualities made him the perfect *male,* not the perfect androgyne.[16] It is recognized in the Orthodox tradition that Christ was truly human, possessing all human qualities, but he still was a male with a masculine relationship toward the Church. This maleness of Christ is neither a passing mode, nor was it incidental (Jn 1:18, 1 Jn 4:9). In addition, it does not contradict his humanity, but is viewed as an *essential* part of that humanity. Jesus Christ had to possess a deep, personal sexuality, or he would not have been fully human and therefore could not have saved the human race (Heb 4:15).

Therefore, the first point of Orthodox christology is that the sex of Jesus was not insignificant or simply biological. The Logos took on a human sexuality, a way of being human, a masculine mode, and he bore this relationship to the Church. He had to assume sexuality as well as every other human

[15]"Sexuality" is used here not in the sense of sexual activity. Jesus had no sexual activity in his life, but he did have a sexuality, a sexual orientation, which was masculine.

[16]Gregory of Nazianzus, *Second Oration on Easter.*

quality or he would not have been the God-human who saves us. The difference between Orthodox Christian doctrine and feminist doctrine is that Orthodox doctrine does not *oppose* the common humanity of Christ to his maleness. "Being human" is possible in two forms: male or female. One is not less human than the other; both women and men have the same human nature, but each is a different form or expression of that humanity. And so it was with Jesus Christ. The traditional Orthodox viewpoint is that Christ assumed human nature common to women and men, but also assumed one of the two ways of being human—the masculine mode.

More importantly, the sex of Jesus was not temporary. Jesus Christ rose from the dead in a male body. It is true that St. Paul in 2 Corinthians 3:17 and 1 Corinthians 15:45 identifies the risen Christ as a "Spirit." Yet, according to Jewish thought:

> This Christ certainly is no impersonal fluid. Even when St. Paul is considering Christ or his body as the sphere of life in which the believer is born and grows, he does not think of that body as an immaterial substance: it always remains in his thought the physical body of the Savior. The Resurrection is produced by a divine action indicated by the verb "ἐγείρειν" (to rouse from sleep). He who "rises up" ("ἀνίστασθαι"), he who is woken up, is the same as he who lay down in the sleep of death: "He was buried and rose again the third day."[17]

The idea that the body falls asleep in hope of the resurrection indicates that the risen person does not lose the status of being female or male. Rather, the whole person (in the traditional Christian sense)—spirit, soul and body—becomes "quickened by the Spirit." As F.X. Durrwell states: "We have found nothing in our text that denies the materiality of the body of the risen Christ, but a confirmation of I

[17]F.X. Durrwell, *The Resurrection* (New York: Sheed and Ward, 1960) 101.

Corinthians 15:45: 'The New Adam was made into a quicken-
ing spirit.' "[18]

The doctrine that the Lord rises in bodily form is essential
to Christian salvation. If Christ had not risen and his flesh
had not been glorified, there would be no possibility of communion between God and humanity. Christ had to take our
humanity *in his body* to heaven.

> The ultimate aim of the divine plan is thus man's
> deification: that whole people might participate in
> the whole God (Θεὸς ὅλος ὅλοις μετεχόμενος),
> and that in the same way in which the soul and body
> are united, God should become partakable of by the
> soul, and by the soul's intermediary, by the body, in
> order that the soul might receive an unchanging char-
> acter and the body, immortality; and finally, that the
> whole man should become God; deified by the grace of
> God become man, becoming whole man, soul and
> body, by nature, and becoming whole God, soul and
> body, by grace.[19]

By denying the bodily resurrection of Jesus Christ in order
to negate his eternal relation to a male body and his masculine
relationship to the Church, feminist theologians also deny
an eternal, deified existence for humanity. For, as St. Paul
wrote, "if Christ has not been raised, your faith is futile and
you are still in your sins" (1 Co 15:17). To negate the
resurrection of the body cuts at the heart of Christian doctrine
and leads to a vision of the afterlife in which humanity is
not saved, since the two essential elements of being human
(soul and body) are disunited. Feminist theologians are
wrong to assume that the resurrection of the soul alone was
the plan for salvation Jesus had in mind when he underwent
death for our sake (1 Co 15:51-55, 15:26). A vision of the
resurrected soul without a resurrected body is not within
traditionally Christian bounds.

Feminist theologians have proposed christologies opposed

---

[18]Ibid., 103.
[19]St. Maximus the Confessor, quoted in Meyendorff, 143.

to God's plan for salvation. They deny Christ's human sexuality (and therefore full, true humanity) and his bodily resurrection in order to make persuasive arguments for the female priesthood. They have claimed that the sex of Jesus Christ was an insignificant, temporary biological state and envision him as a symbol of wholeness which human beings must imitate. These assertions about sexuality are not only opposed to Christian doctrine, they also are extracted directly from the philosophy of the women's movement.

A Feminist Vision of Humanity: An Androgynous World

In the beginning of the women's movement, feminists envisioned a new human community, and new approaches to human sexuality came to the fore. Feminists advocated the avoidance of cultural stereotypes and emphasized personal individuality—the freedom for women and men to adopt both masculine and feminine attitudes and roles. Men were encouraged to develop qualities that had been defined by society as "feminine," such as gentleness; women were encouraged to develop what had been formerly viewed as "masculine" traits, such as assertiveness. Both women and men were encouraged to develop their human characteristics that had been suppressed by cultural taboos, and thus to become "whole" or "androgynous" human beings.[20]

Thus, Friedan, along with successive feminists, perceived the women's movement at its base as a movement within the psyche of each woman (and man). To be liberated meant to look deep within oneself, to determine what, because of the surrounding patriarchal culture, one was suppressing, and to allow those repressed feelings to surface into conscious awareness, where one could deal with them intelligibly and openly. Feminists asserted that people had been conditioned by a male-dominated society to fit into certain stereotyped roles that oppressed and depressed them. Therefore, in order to liberate themselves from inner chaos, people should undergo

[20]Mary Daly, *Beyond God the Father: Toward the Philosophy of Women's Liberation* (Boston: Beacon Press, 1973) 15 *et passim.*

a psychic journey to wholeness and androgyny, recapturing all the human attitudes they had been repressing.[21] Only those who had broken across stereotyped existence, only the woman or man mentally liberated from patriarchal norms, could be called truly whole. According to this early androgynous vision for humanity, life would increasingly require that "individuals know how to take the initiative and to be receptive, to be aggressive and sensitive, to discipline and to nurture, to be both strong and gentle, and so forth, combining what have been defined in American society as masculine and feminine qualities."[22] The more one approximated this in one's life, the more wholly human one became.

If this were the extent of the androgynous vision, of course, it would not be objectionable to the traditional Christian.[23] Indeed, it would even be welcome, since traditional Christians concur that women and men are "consubstantial" in their human nature; both males and females possess all human traits, characteristics and emotions (Gn 1:27-28). There is a common humanity. Women in the Bible certainly do not fit into stereotyped roles. Deborah was a prophetess who judged the people of Israel (Jg 4:4). The glory of war belonged to a woman, Jael (Jg 4:9ff). Queen Esther fixed religious holidays to be celebrated by the Jews (Est 9:29ff). Judith was brave above all the men of Israel (Jdt 13:18-20). Likewise, women of the New Testamental community were not considered subhuman or unfit for salvation (Lk 10:38-42, 1:47-48; Ac 17:4; Ph 4:3). Furthermore, men in the Bible were not always stereotyped according to certain attitudes. For example, King David was capable of a deep love for another man (1 Sm 20:17), and of mercy (1 Sm 24:16-18)

---

[21]This psychic journey is described in the methodology of C.G. Jung (1870-1961). Although Jung sometimes sex-links characteristics of men and women and is therefore unacceptable to some feminists, his description of coming into psychic wholeness is applauded by many feminists. See Burghardt, 185.

[22]Burghardt, 158ff.

[23]"Traditional Christian" will refer in this article to one who believes in the doctrines of the Orthodox Christian Church and her tradition. The term is not interchangeable with "fundamentalist Christian" and is not to be linked with the stereotyped philosophy advocated by some fundamentalists—e.g., Marabel Morgan, The Total Woman (New York: Pocket Books, 1973). Pages 116-7 in particular would be objectionable.

and of tenderness (2 Sm 1:11-12). Therefore, a traditional Christian would not believe that some emotions are reserved for women and others for men. Both are equally human, and possess the whole of human traits.

The problem is that, with time, "psychic wholeness" or "androgyny" came to be more rigidly defined by feminists. "Androgyny" began to imply that psychologically there are *no* distinctions between women and men; anatomy alone distinguishes the sexes. Without bodily form, and considering only psychic identity, it would be impossible to distinguish between women and men.[24] There is no existent complementarity between the sexes; in the spiritual realm, the two distinct forms of humanity—female and male—would not exist. Those who saw androgyny as the ideal vision for humanity emphasized similarities between the sexes without reference to psychological differences.[25] They blamed culture for setting up sexual distinctions, and sought to reeducate women and men that the only difference between them was anatomical.

Unfortunately, feminized-Christians accepted this extreme androgynous vision from the secular women's movement and used it extensively in their theology. Feminist theologians began to stress common humanity and psychic similarity between women and men at the expense of distinction or complementarity between the sexes. They also began to theorize that the difference between women and men was purely anatomical and would be overcome in heaven. They began to predict that in the reign of God there would be "neither male nor female" (their interpretation of Ga 3:28), and that meanwhile, on earth, humanity should be working toward the effacement of sexual distinction in cooperation with the Holy Spirit.[26] Indeed, they began to emphasize humanity, liberation, human wholeness, androgyny and asexuality. The following quotations illustrate this exchange between feminist philosophers and feminist theologians.

Feminist authors Rosemary Radford Ruether and Eleanor

[24]Burghardt, 159.
[25]Ibid.
[26]Rosemary Ruether and Eleanor McLaughlin, eds., *Women of Spirit* (New York: Simon and Schuster, 1979) 23.

McLaughlin state in their coedited work, *Women of Spirit,*
that in the age to come, all sexual distinction will be abolished; and in the spiritual life, this effacement already occurs:
"through holiness and ecstasy a woman transcends 'nature'
and participates in the eschatological sphere. She anticipates
the order of salvation of heaven. In this eschatological order,
sexual hierarchy is abolished for that asexual personhood in
which there is 'neither male nor female.' "[27]

Likewise, Alla Bozarth-Campbell and Carter Heywood,
two women who were ordained to the Episcopalian priesthood
in 1974, also accept feminism as a type of Christian spirituality and androgyny as the goal for humanity. Heywood states:

> If my first year at seminary had been marked by trauma,
> this second year was graced by rapid growth which I
> myself could feel even as it set in. I can attribute this
> growth to two simultaneous and complementary pro-
> cesses: psychotherapy and a woman's consciousness
> raising group, from both of which I initially shied
> away and each of which landed me near the heart of
> the Christian faith: a realization of my own being's
> movement in harmony with that of the Holy Spirit.[28]

Heywood also prays that the Holy Spirit will redeem Christian
communities so that they "will more faithfully reflect God's
design for the liberation and wholeness of each human being
in the world."[29] In addition, Heywood admits it was the
feminist spirituality that led her to the vocation of the priesthood and sanctioned it.[30]

Similarly, Bozarth-Campbell refers to the "wholemaking"
feminist ideology several times in her book, *Womanpriest:
A Personal Odyssey,* especially in the last chapter, entitled
"God is a Verb."[31] She states that the priesthood itself, in

[27]Ibid.
[28]Carter Heywood, *A Priest Forever* (New York: Harper and Row, 1976)
106.
[29]Ibid.
[30]Ibid., 29.
[31]Alla Bozarth-Campbell, *Womanpriest: A Personal Odyssey* (New York:
Paulist Press, 1978) 198ff.

order to reflect full and whole humanity, liberation and androgyny, should include women. If women are excluded from it, the priesthood would be a symbol not of wholeness but of a dualistic, hierarchical, oppressive system, out of line with a liberated, holistic design for humanity and out of line with the image of the holistic Christ who embodies all of humanity.[32] Moreover, she believes that the priest is not only "father" to the community, but bears multifaceted relationships to it: the priest at times is "mother," "brother" and "sister" as well. She regards the priest as a "person" who can bring various spiritual gifts to the ministry. "Personhood" and individuality are stressed; she denies any distinctions between masculine and feminine vocations.[33]

Another feminist theologian, Una Kroll, states: "Because I am a Christian it is natural that my ideas about wholeness should have derived from a consideration about the person of Christ, who seems to me to have been the most whole person who ever lived."[34]

From these few examples, it is clear that feminized-Christians have borrowed much from feminist philosophy and psychology to provide a support system for the female priesthood.[35] However, as applied to Jesus Christ, this feminist theology has caused severe distortions in christology and soteriology. And as applied to humanity in general, it runs afoul of traditional Christian anthropology as well.

Traditional Christian Anthropology

No traditional Christian could admit that humanity consists of two forms whose *only* distinction is anatomical; a spiritual complementarity between the sexes is assumed as well. Genesis 2:18 states: "Then the Lord God said, 'It is not good that man should be alone; I will make him a helper

[32]Ibid., 168.
[33]Ibid., 167-9.
[34]Kroll, 100.
[35]But cf n. 5 above—some feminist theologians claim that Christian theology influenced feminist philosophy and not vice-versa.

fit for him.' " The word "helper" in this passage has as its Hebrew root *eser kenegdo.* Joan Schaupp, in her book, *Woman: Image of the Holy Spirit,* gives some insight into this word:

> *Vis-à-vis,* the French term meaning face-to-face, is the expression used to capture the meaning of the Hebrew phrase, *eser kenegdo . . . Vis-à-vis* would also have the connotation: counterpart, a mirror, a person created to help man discover himself. Scripture implies, there-fore, that the woman is not a passive or inferior force, but the other half necessary for a mutually enriching dialogue . . . real face-to-face discourse, meaningful contact with women, is probably necessary for a man to achieve an integrated personality. *Eser kenegdo* implies this. For a balanced viewpoint, a male needs women friends, women co-workers, women associates in what-ever his endeavor happens to be. Similarly, women need male associates to develop integrated personali-ties.[36]

It appears that although men and women are equal in honor and equally human, there is a psychological interplay, a complementary relationship between them, which could not be accomplished in an androgynous world where the neces-sary complementarity is suppressed. God's creative act is not complete, not "good" (Gn 2:18), until both forms of human-ity are present and the feminine/masculine complement exists for the enrichment and fulfilment of life. "Androgyny," when taken to the extreme, is an ideal that leaves one not with a sense of wholeness or unity, but of insipidness, because a created relationship has been eradicated.[37] Therefore, although the viewpoint that women and men should be stereotyped

[36] Joan Schaupp, *Woman: Image of the Holy Spirit* (Denville, N.J.: Dimen-sion Books, 1975) 72-3.

[37] This relationship is particularly expressed in the relationship between God and his people, which is akin to the love expressed between a man and a woman (Is 54:5-6, 62:5; Rv 21:9-10). If such love is eradicated or sup-pressed in the human community, creatures de facto will have no experience of one of the ways in which God loves them.

into roles is disturbing to the traditional Christian's vision of humanity, equally disturbing is the extreme feminist viewpoint that sexual complementarity should be denied or perceived as a culturally learned interplay that is actually nonexistent outside of stereotyped social situations.[38]

In the Orthodox tradition, complementarity between sexes is known to be a creative act of God. "Femininity" and "masculinity" are actual human qualities, deeply connected to the person; they are modes of human be-ing, i.e., ways of being human. The terms "masculinity" and "femininity" are not qualifying adjectives of other human traits. (Feminists might consider a shy, sensitive person to be on the "feminine" side, for example, regardless of whether that person is male or female.) Rather, "masculinity" and "femininity" are in themselves necessary human qualities, ways of expressing a personality. Femininity and masculinity are gifts from God to be used in personal expression and behavior.[39]

The traditional anthropological belief concerning women and men is that they together, in complementarity, make up the human community. Each bears a certain relation to the other and to all of humanity. Therefore, spiritual vocations differ, since sexuality is regarded not as insignificant but as being intimately connected to the person—moving in certain directions, shaping behavior and manifesting itself in two forms: either masculine or feminine. Women and men have been endowed with special, distinct ways of expressing a common humanity, and these modes are not exchangeable; masculinity and femininity are not interchangeable.[40]

Further, this created complementarity is not temporary until death, as feminists would have it. We are not "saved"

[38]Daly, 15.

[39]". . . manhood and womanhood give to human nature a different form of existence both spiritually and bodily. It is proper to consider these differences to be relational and functional, but at the same time innate." Serge Verhovskoy, "The Orthodox Understanding of the Relationship between Man and Woman and the Christian Family," unpublished article by the Professor Emeritus of Dogmatic, Moral and Comparative Theology at St. Vladimir's Orthodox Theological Seminary, Crestwood, N.Y.

[40]Paul Tournier, *The Gift of Feeling* (Atlanta: John Knox Press, 1979). Tournier defines the complementarity between women and men without assigning specific roles or stereotyping male and female existence.

from sexual distinction in the resurrection. The feminist expectation that the soul and body, or psychological and physical states, will be dissociated in the heavenly realm is completely foreign to Judeo-Christian thought. The body is not temporary, earthly baggage to be discarded after death. Rather, the resurrection of the body as well as the soul is a fundamental Christian tenet, a condition promised by Jesus Christ.

St. Paul states that after the physical body dies, there is another body which is to be, a spiritual body, a body changed. We will not be disincarnate, but further clothed (2 Co 5:1-3) in immortality. Just as traditional Christians believe Jesus Christ rose from the dead in an incorrupt body, so they hope in the resurrection of their own bodies. Our bodies will be changed, quickened and nourished by the Spirit, made incorruptible, but our bodies will remain. We will be raised as males and females; creation will be restored, not annihilated. This idea, which scandalized the Greeks long ago, may play havoc with the modern mind today; nevertheless it is an essential doctrine of the Christian faith.

Unlike the Platonists and Aristotelian philosophers, Christians always insisted on this union of soul and body even in the afterlife. As the Orthodox theologian Georges Florovsky noted:

> Body belongs originally to the unity of human existence. And this was perhaps the most striking novelty of the original Christian message. The preaching of the Resurrection as well as the preaching of the Cross was foolishness and a stumbling block to the Gentiles. The Greek mind was always rather disgusted with the body. The attitude of the average Greek in the early Christian times was strongly influenced by Platonic and Orphic ideas, and it was a common opinion that the body was a kind of "prison" in which the fallen soul was incarcerated and confined. The Greeks dreamt rather of a complete and final disincarnation.[41]

[41]Georges Florovsky, *Creation and Redemption*, Collected Works, 3 (Belmont, Mass.: Nordland, 1976) 115.

And concerning the integrity of the soul and body on earth, he wrote:

> For man is originally composed of body and soul. Neither soul nor body separately represents man. A body without a soul is but a corpse, and a soul without a body is a ghost . . . Mysterious as the union of soul and body indeed is, the immediate consciousness of man witnesses to the organic wholeness of his psychophysical structure. This organic wholeness was from the very beginning strongly emphasized by all Christian teachers.[42]

It is apparent that traditional Christians believe several things about human sexuality that feminist theologians do not. The traditional Christian believes in an eternal, created complementarity between the sexes, in a bodily resurrection and in an intimate correlation between the psychical and the biological state of a person. Several Orthodox theologians even have maintained that the body is an outward reflection of the soul; they are closely connected.[43]

For an Orthodox Christian, sexual distinction is not insignificant, merely biological, or temporary; it is *significant, psychological* and *biological,* and *permanent.* By denying this Orthodox teaching, feminist theologians also deny a creative act of God—the creation of two complementary forms of humanity—and a salvific act of God—the bodily resurrection in which all early Christians believed and hoped.

The Holy Trinity

The names for God and the vision of the Holy Trinity constitute the final point of contention between feminized-

[42]Ibid., 106.

[43]Georges Florovsky, *Aspects of Church History,* Collected Works, 4 (Belmont, Mass.: Nordland, 1976) 96. Patristic sources, however, vary on this subject. St. Gregory of Nyssa, for example, states that "the soul is the inward image of the body" (quoted in Florovsky, *Creation and Redemption,* 124), yet in another instance he declares that the only distinguishable difference between a male and a female is in the body and not in the soul.

Christians and Orthodox Christians. Feminist theologians in general object to the traditional terms for God—Father, Son and Holy Spirit—because, they say, such terms connote maleness and alienate women from the Church and God. In addition, these terms leave women feeling inferior to men in the Christian community and excluded from its worship. Moreover, the fact that terms for God connote a masculinity has had sociological ramifications: women have become third in a succession of power—God, males, and then females.

Therefore, feminized-Christians have proposed other terms for God: either nonpersonal ones, such as "Fire, Light, Almighty"; terms denoting actions, such as "Savior, Creator, Comforter"; or terms with feminine connotations, such as "Mother" and "She."[44] Using such terms, they claim, will enrich the image of God, as well as balance the masculine image of God with a feminine one. Bozarth-Campbell explains:

> . . . we speak of the Persons of the Trinity as Creator, Savior and Sanctifier, *emphasizing the aspects of God's activity rather than the one-sided sexual imagery devised by the patriarchy.* In the Creed, the transcendence of God is recognized in the First Person of the Creator, who is beyond gender; the immanent masculine is recognized in the human person of Jesus (though not necessarily in the eternal Christ, the Creative Word); and the immanent feminine is celebrated in the Holy Spirit, the Giver of Life.[45]

In her trinitarian formula, Bozarth-Campbell has tried to include masculine, feminine and immanent and transcendent elements in order to provide humanity with a palatable Christian God, rather than with what she views as a patriarchal formula for God.

[44]The United Church of Christ has published a booklet encouraging the avoidance of traditional trinitarian language and suggesting several alternatives for names for God. See *Inclusive Language Guidelines for Use and Study in the United Church of Christ* (St. Louis: UCC, Church Leadership Resources, 1980).
    [45]Bozarth-Campbell, 214.

Such efforts by feminized-Christians to change terms for God are directly related to the female priesthood. Feminist theologians feel that such changes will open up the Christian community to the inclusion of women on all levels of ministration. A God cast in male-female imagery or impersonal imagery would do much to effect changes in attitudes toward women in the community. However, from the Orthodox Christian viewpoint, such changes in the terms for God lead to distortion of the image of the Trinity and also border on heresy.

First, from the Orthodox standpoint, it is inadequate (although not incorrect) to describe God either with nonpersonal terms such as "Beauty, Light, Life" *alone* or with terms denoting a function, such as "Creator, Savior and Sanctifier." This is because God is a *personal being,* and to deny the personal aspect of the three members of the Trinity leads to a mistaken image of God. God is not just goodness and perfection; God is three persons in a union. Such a personal doctrine of the Holy Trinity allows for the closest relationship between God and creatures. As the Orthodox theologian Vladimir Lossky states:

> [God] is a personal Absolute who enters into relationships with human persons. For Judaism before Christ, as for a believing Jew today, this is so. To quote the witness of Martin Buber: "The great achievement of Israel is not to have taught the one true God, who is the only God, the source and end of all that is; it is to have shown that it was possible *in reality* to speak to Him, to say, 'Thou' to Him, to stand upright before His face." "It was Israel who first understood and—much more—lived life as a dialogue between man and God."[46]

Ultimately, the tendency of feminized-Christians to proclaim God as utmost "Beauty, Light, Life," although not incorrect, leads to a depersonalized image of God. Three per-

[46]Vladimir Lossky, *In the Image and Likeness of God* (Crestwood, N.Y.: SVS Press, 1974) 129.

sons are not denoted by such terms, only qualities or characteristics. This is a serious theological error. It leads to abstrac-
tion in imaging God, and to the widespread tendency in contemporary Christianity to describe God in a rather unclear
manner—"God is Big, God is Fire, God is Wind"—without
ever considering that the New Testament records that God
has been revealed as *three persons.* Feminist theologians accept some qualities of God without ever acknowledging what
Jesus Christ proclaimed: God is "Father, Son and Holy
Spirit" (Jn 14:26, 15:26). In addition, a personal God provides for creatures a pattern to imitate. One can know what
true personhood is by understanding the community of God
in three persons.[47] To exchange a personal God for imagery
of *qualities* of God leads to inadequate conceptions of God
and depersonalization of both God and humanity.

A functional God—"Creator, Savior, Sanctifier"—is just as
inadequate, because again the persons of the Trinity are in-
sufficiently defined. By reviewing Bozarth-Campbell's proposal, one notes that the trinitarian image becomes distorted.
This is because, according to Scripture, the persons of the
Trinity perform *all* functions *in concert:* they *all* create (Jn
1:1-3, Gn 1:2), they *all* effect salvation (Acts 2:24, Rm
1:4), they *all* sanctify (Eph 5:26, 1 Th 5:23). According to
the Bible, it is impossible to distinguish between members
of the Trinity by what *they do,* since functionally they act
together in their economical actions toward creatures. Gregory
of Nyssa notes this in his discussion of the term "Comforter."
Even the word "Comforter," he says, is not a term for the
Holy Spirit alone, "for David says to the Father, 'Thou,
Lord, hast holpen me and comforted me' (Ps 76:17), and
the great apostle applies to the Father the same language
when he says, 'Blessed be the God and Father of our Lord
Jesus Christ, who comforts us in all our tribulation' (2 Co
1:3-4)."[48] A trinitarian formula such as the one given by
Bozarth-Campbell does nothing to tell *who God is,* only *what*

---

[47]Orthodox theologians meditate on the icon of the Holy Trinity (depict-
ing the three angels sent to Abraham—Gn 18:1-8) in defining the paradigm
for the perfection of the relationships in the human community.
[48]Gregory of Nyssa, *Against Eunomius* 2.

God does toward creatures; and since the three persons of
God perform all functions toward creatures together, such a
formula is inadequate to define three persons in God. Which
is the Creator? Which is the Savior? Which is the Sanctifier?
One cannot describe God by function alone; the trinitarian
character of God becomes confused by such terms.

Neither the qualifying names nor the functional names
for God proposed by feminists, although not entirely incorrect, denote a well-defined image of a trinitarian God. The
Orthodox Church insists on personal names. However, it
must be stated, then, why the terms "Father," "Son" and
"Holy Spirit" were chosen and used instead of the feminist
terms "Mother," "Parent" and "She."

The Most Adequate Terms

There were two fourth-century Orthodox theologians, St.
Athanasius and St. Gregory of Nyssa, who were embroiled in
controversies over the subject of terms for God, and their
arguments would be worthwhile study for feminist theologians today. The dispute over the terms for God in fact is
age-old, and by studying these two one can see that the terms
"Father, Son and Holy Spirit" were not used by the Church
to magnify maleness; they were not part of a patriarchal ploy
to keep women "in place." They were theological terms used
to describe the *inner relationships* among members of the
Trinity, and to describe as well as humanly possible the unknowable, ineffable Godhead.

Athanasius was defending the traditional trinitarian names
against a group that called the first person of the Trinity
"Creator" rather than "Father." These people clung to the
Arian heresy, which claimed that Jesus Christ was not the
Son of God but merely a superior creature, and therefore
"Father" was a fleshly, foolish, improper term for God.[49] In
discussing the subject, Athanasius tried to illustrate the im-
portance of the biblical divine names "Father, Son and Holy

[49]For an explanation of this heresy, see Philip Schaff, *History of the Christian Church* 3 (Grand Rapids, Mich.: Eerdmans, 1910) 618-49.

Spirit." He argued that the term "Creator" described only a divine action of God toward creatures, and even made the existence of God dependent on creation. "If creation did not exist," he asked, "would this 'Creator God' cease to be? If creation never existed, what would be the proper term for God?"

Athanasius argued that the names of God had to describe more than his will or action. God could be called "Maker," "Helper," "Defender" or a number of other names, but these terms only described actions; they were not adequate to describe the members of the Trinity as they relate to one another without reference to creation or creatures. The persons themselves must be given other, personal names. He therefore insisted that one use the terms "Father, Son and Holy Spirit" when speaking about the existence of God as three persons in a community of love, the relationships among the Trinity and God's *very being* (ontological existence). "God's 'Being' has an absolute ontological priority over God's action and will. *God is much more than just 'Creator.' When we call God 'Father' we mean something higher than his relation to creatures."*[50]

"There are, as it were, two different sets of names which may be used for God," explained Athanasius. "One set (Creator, Savior, Sanctifier) refers to God's deeds or acts—that is, to his will and counsel—the other (Father, Son and Holy Spirit) to God's own essence and being." Athanasius insisted that these two sets be formally and consistently distinguished.[51]

St. Gregory of Nyssa faced similar problems when dealing with a sect known as the Eunomians, who believed that Christ was unlike God the Father by nature and instead was a created energy. For this reason the Eunomians refused to call God "Father." Gregory, appalled by this new teaching, sought to explain the character of the Holy Trinity, the relationships among the persons of the Trinity and the Church's insistence upon the traditional terms "Father, Son and Holy

[50]Athanasius, *Against the Arians* 1:3, quoted in Florovsky, *Aspects of Church History*, 52. Emphasis is mine.
[51]Florovsky, *Aspects of Church History*, 52.

Spirit." Most importantly, Gregory taught that a deviation from these traditional terms causes deviations in doctrine. If one does not use these precise theological terms, he warned, an unclear image of the reality of the Trinity emerges, a misguided conception occurs, one contemplates a mistaken impression of God. Any terms other than "Father, Son and Holy Spirit," he said, "serve as a starting point for the deflection of sound doctrine."[52]

First of all, said Gregory, there was no more adequate theologian than the Lord himself, who without compulsion or misdirection designated the Godhead as "Father, Son and Holy Spirit."[53] Further, these names are not indications that God is man or male (any Orthodox theologian would be shocked by such a deduction), for God transcends human gender.[54] Rather, they imply relationships among the persons of the Trinity, and distinguish them as separate persons who yet exist in a community of love. Even more crucial, the names lead one to contemplate the correct relationships among the three persons, and their particular personalities and modes of existence.

The name "Father," said Gregory, leads one to contemplate two things: a being who is the source and cause of all, and the fact that this being has a relationship with another person—for one can only be "Father" if there is a child involved.[55] Thus, the term "Father" leads one naturally to think of another member of the Trinity, to contemplate more than is suggested by "Creator" or "Maker." By calling God "Father," notes Gregory, one understands that there exists with him a Child from all eternity, a second person who is coruling, coequal and coeternal with him.[56] There never was a time when the source of all, the Father, was not in relationship as Father to the second divine being (Jn 1:1). "Father" also connotes the initiator of a generation, the inaugurator of all, the one who begets life rather than bringing it to

[52]Gregory of Nyssa, *Against Eunomius* 2:9.
[53]Ibid., 1.
[54]Gregory of Nazianzus notes that the names of God have nothing whatsoever to do with sexuality. *Fifth Oration* 7.
[55]Gregory of Nyssa, *Against Eunomius* 1.
[56]Ibid., 4:1.

fruition in birth.[57] This is the mode of existence (the way of being) of the first person of the Trinity. How he acts in trinitarian life, his relationship to the other two divine beings, is akin to the mode of existence of a father in the earthly realm.

Likewise, the word "Son" carries with it certain connotations: that he is begotten by another being and is of the same divine nature as that being. In addition, the word "Son" implies a close affinity between the two beings, a love-relationship. As Scripture states, the Son is given life by the Father (Jn 5:26); he is the "express image of the Father" (Col 1:15); he is "the brightness of the glory of the Father" (Heb 1:3).[58] In the incarnation, and resurrection, the child is revealed as the eternal Son (Jn 1:18).

The term "Holy Spirit" implies two things by its dual name. "Holy" implies that there is another person of the Trinity who shares in the holiness of the Father and Son, and thereby is equally divine. "Spirit," on the other hand, connotes a personification. A "spirit" is necessarily the spirit *of* someone else; the "Spirit" personifies the life of the Father. As Gregory says: "since the appellation of 'Spirit,' and that of 'Holy,' are equally applied by the Scriptures to the Father and to the Son—for 'God is a Spirit' [Jn 4:24], and 'the anointed Lord is the Spirit before our face' [Lm 4:20 in the Septuagint], and the 'Lord our God is holy' [Ps 99:9], and there is 'one holy, one Lord Jesus Christ'—this leads one to contemplate a third person who shares in life and holiness equally with the Father and the Son from all eternity."[59]

---

[57]Feminists argue that woman, as well as man, is the source of all life, and therefore this first person of the Holy Trinity may be called "Mother" as well as "Father." However, at the basic biological level, the interaction between a male sperm and a female ovum still reveals a distinction of action. The early Church was well aware that it took both male and female cells to create life, and that the male was not the only creator of life (see John Chrysostom, *Homily 20 on Ephesians* 5). The Church, however, always maintained a distinction between begetting and bearing, between the male and female contributions and modes of action in creating life. The male cell is the generator, inaugurator and impregnator; there are distinctions in the biological act of creation.

[58]Gregory of Nyssa, *Against Eunomius* 1:39.

[59]Ibid., 2:22.

Gregory's points are these: there are three persons of God, of the same divine nature, who are in relationship from all eternity; so close is their relationship and bond of love that the contemplation of one leads to the perception of the other two. Moreover, these three persons relate to each other in different manners. There is polarity and variety in their relationships. Each person has a unique manner or mode of existence, and a unique relationship to the other two.[60] The terms "Father, Son and Holy Spirit" lead us to contemplate these relationships and unique personalities. They were not used, as feminized-Christians would have us believe, to project an image of a male God.

Gregory's contemplation of the Trinity is much more sublime than that of the feminists. Feminized-Christians contemplate the Trinity in relationship to creatures, for they advocate the use of terms relative *to us*. Gregory, on the other hand, urges us to contemplate the mystery of the Trinity, in itself, the relationships *among the three persons* who have existed from all eternity. This is the Trinity out of which flows love (1 Jn 4:8), and which is revealed to us as three persons in one divine essence through the revelation in the New Testament in the Spirit of the Church.

These traditional titles, states the Orthodox Church, are best able to lead to the correct and precise knowledge of the Trinity. Gregory proclaims, "our Master Christ . . . commits us these titles as better able to bring us to faith about the Self-Existent, declaring that it suffices us to cling to the titles 'Father, Son and Holy Spirit' in order to attain to the apprehension of him who is absolutely existent, who is one and yet not one."[61] Although no human words are adequate to describe God entirely, these words given to us by the Lord are the most adequate that can be found.

Still, feminized-Christians might protest on the grounds that "Father, Son and Holy Spirit" *in contemporary society* do not connote what they did in Gregory's or Athanasius' time. Moreover, say feminist theologians, there are many instances in Scripture in which God is cast in a feminine role

[60]Ibid., 1:22.
[61]Ibid., 2:2.

—why not then call God "Mother"? (Is 46:3-4, Ps 131:1-2, Lk 13:34)

An Orthodox Christian might respond positively that *toward us creatures* God indeed acts like a kind, merciful mother, always willing to forgive the disobedience of her children and to comfort them. However, when speaking of trinitarian relationships, one should again revert to the use of the term "Father." The poetic language of referring to God as "Mother" should not be substituted for the precise theological terminology of calling God "Father," or else confusion will result.[62]

By an exegesis of two more scriptural passages, the Orthodox Christian Church's insistence on calling God "Father" will be made more clear: "For this reason I bow my knees before the Father, from whom every fatherhood [πατριά] in heaven and on earth is named" (Eph 3:14-15). "And call no man your father on earth, for you have one Father, who is in heaven" (Mt 23:9).

The first passage, from St. Paul, implies that God is the one, true, divine Father whom human fathers imitate in some creaturely, transient way. Orthodox Christians do not call God "Father" to justify a patriarchal culture. Rather, males in a human household are called "fathers" because they imitate and reflect the image of the heavenly "Father," albeit in a human, creaturely way. That is, a heavenly "Father" exists as an objective reality that *transcends* human fatherhood and the male sex, but nevertheless it is the human father and not the human mother who imitates and is a reflection of this particular mode of being. The act of generation between a human father and child and the act of generation between the divine Father and Child is analogous, as far as divine-human relationships can be.

[62]There are many patristic as well as mystical writings in which God is viewed as a mother, both in the Eastern Orthodox tradition and in the western tradition. For example, St. Therese of Lisieux, a Roman Catholic nun of the Carmelite order, wrote in the nineteenth century: "I know that God loves us more tenderly than any mother, and is a mother not always ready to forgive the involuntary failings of her child?" Christopher O'Mahoney, ed., *St. Therese of Lisieux by Those who Knew Her* (Huntington, Ind.: Our Sunday Visitor, 1975) 43. However, in such instances the authors reflect on the kindness and compassion of God; God is not named "Mother."

Perhaps it would be more clear to say that the generative
force of the Father in trinitarian life is imitated by males
and not females on earth.[63] In the second scriptural passage,
taken from Matthew, Jesus Christ implies this, but also
describes the wide difference between earthly and divine
fatherhood. The Lord recognized that the Fatherhood of God
was fatherhood in its total, divine, perfect form, and that
human fatherhood could be at best only a partial analogy to
this supreme divine act. Yet Jesus consistently called God
"Father" and not "Mother." The passage from Matthew also
indicates, then, that although human and divine fatherhood
are worlds apart, Jesus viewed God as substantially *Father*.
His very being was fatherhood personified. Before time, in
the mystery of the Holy Trinity, the Father generated a Son.
Therefore, the best human term possible to describe this
eternal, divine, generative action was that chosen by Jesus
Christ: "Father."[64]

This divine Father is as different from and transcendent
of earthly fathers as the divine is of the human. Nevertheless
it is fatherhood and not motherhood which describes his
mode of life, his relationship to the second person of the
Trinity and, through adoption by Jesus Christ, his relationship
to us. The first person of the Trinity does not just "act" like
a father (though he sometimes acts like a mother!), but
rather his very being is divine fatherhood in a pure, eternal,
fulfilled state. Fatherhood is a *function* of males on earth,
but for the first person of the Trinity, it is the *principle* of
his being.[65] It is what distinguishes him from the other two
members of the Trinity.[66]

All of this does not mean, of course, that Orthodox
theologians have not recognized a reflection of a "feminine"
element in the Godhead as well. God is beyond human sex-

[63]Cf above, n. 57.

[64]Louis Bouyer, *Woman in the Church* (San Francisco: Ignatius Press,
1979) 29-32.

[65]Ibid., 32.

[66]Gregory of Nazianzus, *On the Holy Spirit*. Gregory explains how the
names of God reveal the distinguishing characteristics of the members of the
Trinity. The fact that the first person is ungenerate yet generates another
person distinguishes him as "Father."

uality, but, interestingly enough, in the Orthodox Christian
tradition there has been a tendency to identify the Holy Spirit
with womanhood, and certainly there is evidence as such in
Scripture.[67] Orthodox theologians have made analogies between the male/female relationship in the human realm and
the Son/Spirit relationship in the Trinity. The Son's mode of
life and way of relating to the Spirit is viewed as the prototype for masculine behavior; the Spirit's mode of existence
and way of relating to the Son is seen as the prototype for
feminine behavior. Fr. Thomas Hopko notes:

> I believe that God created human beings according to
> his own image and likeness because of the trinitarian
> character of the Divine Nature, and that *the proper
> interrelationship between the sexes within the order of
> creation is patterned after the interrelationship between
> God's Son and his Spirit* . . . the Godhead is not merely
> a "unity" but a "union." Within this "union" there is
> a definite "order" of relationships, which is perfectly
> divine, yet which includes a distinction of "personal
> modes of existence" in which the Son and the Spirit
> have a definite form of relationship . . . Christ is the
> King and the Spirit is Kingship. Christ is the Anointed
> and the Spirit is the Unction. Christ is the Head and
> the Spirit fills his body. Christ is the Bridegroom, and
> the Spirit dwells in his Bride. And Christ and the Spirit
> are perfectly one in their inseparable unity in God,
> who is love.[68]

Likewise, Vladimir Lossky states:

> The Fathers relate the procession of the Holy Spirit
> with what they call the "procession" of Eve, different
> from Adam yet of the same nature as him: unity of
> nature and plurality of persons evoke for us the
> mysteries of the New Testament. Just as the Spirit is

[67]Schaupp, *passim;* Bouyer, 37-9.
[68]Thomas Hopko, *The Spirit of God* (Wilton, Conn.: Morehouse-Barlow,
1976) 49. Emphasis is mine.

not inferior to Him from Whom it proceeds, just so woman is not inferior to man: for love demands equality and love alone wished this primordial polarization, source of all diversity of the human species.[69]

These authors suggest that there is a relationship and polarity between the Son and Spirit, or the Father and the Spirit, which, in the human realm, is manifested as polarity in male/female relationships. This is not to assign sexuality to the Godhead, but rather different modalities to women and men. The Father is not a male and the Spirit is not a female. But females and males in relationship on earth are a reflection of divine relationships.

Curiously, not all feminist theologians disagree with this Orthodox Christian contemplation of the Holy Spirit. Many see the Holy Spirit as an archetypal pattern for womanhood. Rachel Wahlburg, of the Lutheran Church in America, wrote in *The Women's Creed:*

> I believe in the Holy Spirit
> The Woman Spirit of God
> Who like a hen
> Created us
> And gave us birth
> And covers us
> With her wings. . . .[70]

Bozarth-Campbell also refers to the Holy Spirit as "she" in the creed used by her community.[71]

Therefore, in contemplating the third person of the Trinity, feminist theologians and Orthodox theologians have a point of possible agreement. However, the fact that feminized-Christians have dismissed the traditional terms for the Trinity as patriarchal plans for the subordination of women has caused a deep rift between the two theologies.

[69]Vladimir Lossky, *Orthodox Theology: An Introduction* (Crestwood, N.Y.: SVS Press, 1978) 69-70.
[70]Published in *Jesus and the Freed Woman* (New York: Paulist Press, 1978).
[71]Bozarth-Campbell, 215.

Conclusion

The ordination of women has been supported by a christology, anthropology and trinitarian theology in opposition
to that taught by Scripture, church tradition and Jesus Christ
himself. The prediction of Friedan has come to pass: the
greatest impact of the women's movement has been in the
realm of theology.

Women certainly must not be prevented from using their
gifts in the Church—as teachers, theologians, counselors,
missionaries, monastics, musicians, preachers. The Church
should bless, recognize and grant authority to women in the
traditional ordained orders of service to the poor, sick or
unlearned, such as deaconesses, widows and virgins of the
past used to render.[72] Women baptized and chrismated within
the Church have received salvation in Jesus Christ and gifts
of the Holy Spirit to be exercised within the Church without
regard to gender.

However, in the Orthodox Christian sense, the priesthood
is not one of the gifts of the Holy Spirit (1 Co 12) given in
chrismation. Women *or* men are not necessarily guaranteed
it at their baptism; the sacramental priesthood is open to
only *some* men and no women, according to the tradition of
the Church.[73] Not by gifts for preaching, healing, teaching,
prophecy or counseling are priests chosen. To be ordained a
priest rather means to have the Holy Spirit come upon a man
to make and confirm him as the one in the community who
presents the priesthood of Jesus Christ to the rest of the community. It means, by the mystery of the Spirit, to bear the
presence of, not to *represent,* the priesthood of Jesus Christ
at the altar and in all the sacraments of the Church. This
"bearing" is not something the priest can "own" or call his
"gift," since it is a gift given by the Lord to the Church and
for the Church until he comes again.[74] The priesthood entails

[72]Roger Gryson, *The Ministry of Women in the Early Church* (Collegeville, Minn.: Liturgical Press, 1976) *passim.*
[73]Graham Neville, tr., *St. John Chrysostom: Six Books on the Priesthood*
(Crestwood, N.Y.: SVS Press, 1977) 54.
[74]Thomas Hopko, "On the Male Character of the Christian Priesthood"
(see above, 119).

bearing a certain mode of existence toward the Church, a relationship dependent on a certain sexuality.

Such an explanation may seem unjust or ludicrous to feminized-Christians. The support for the ordination of women and the feminist theology that buttresses it is swelling among Protestants and Roman Catholics.[75] Because feminist theologians do not distinguish between masculine and feminine vocations in general, they can see no theological reason for not ordaining women.

Yet, the Orthodox Christian Church, in view of the theology propagated by feminized-Christians, must stand against this trend. The Church instead must defend truly biblical definitions of God, woman and man; she must defend the image of the Lord Jesus Christ and the meaning of ordination; and she must walk according to the light of the Lord (1 Jn 1:6-7). A phenomenon that has caused such distortions in Christian theology cannot be defended by the Orthodox Church.

[75]"No Pause on Women Priests—But Caution on Women Bishops," *Church Times* (August 18, 1978) 10; Professor Lampe and Deaconess McClatchy, "A Consideration of Some of the Historical Objections to the Ordination of Women," a contributing paper to the debate on the female priesthood held at All Souls Langham Place, January 1978, p. 4.

Acknowledgment is made to the authors and publishers of the following works, which have been quoted in this article:

Flesh of my Flesh, by Una Kroll, published and copyrighted 1975 by Darton, Longman and Todd, Ltd., London. Used by permission of the publishers.

The Resurrection, by F.X. Durrwell, published and copyrighted 1960 by Sheed and Ward, New York. Used by permission of the publishers.

Womanpriest: A Personal Odyssey, by Alla Bozarth-Campbell, published by Paulist Press, New York, and copyrighted 1978 by Alla Bozarth-Campbell. Used by permission of the author.

Aspects of Church History: Volume Four in the Collected Works of Georges Florovsky and *Creation and Redemption: Volume Three in the Collected Works of Georges Florovsky,* by Georges Florovsky, published and copyrighted 1975 by Nordland Publishing Company, 85 Evergreen Way, Belmont, Mass. 02178. Used by permission of the publishers.

A Priest Forever, by Carter Heywood, published and copyrighted 1976 by Harper & Row, New York. Used by permission of the publishers.

It Changed my Life, by Betty Friedan, published and copyrighted 1963 by Random House, Inc., New York. Used by permission of the publishers.

Women and the Priesthood:
Reflections on the Debate

By Thomas Hopko

Within the vast body of literature on the subject of women and the priesthood, two books stand out for special attention by the Orthodox. One is a collection of essays by Roman Catholic scholars, entitled *Women and Priesthood: Future Directions. A Call to Dialogue from the Faculty of the Catholic Theological Union at Chicago.*[1] The other, *The Ordination of Women: An Essay on the Office of Christian Ministry,*[2] is by the Protestant "evangelical" theologian Paul K. Jewett. These books are important for the Orthodox because both call for the ordination of women for theological reasons drawn from Scripture and tradition.[3]

On October 15, 1976, the Roman Catholic Church's Sacred Congregation for the Doctrine of Faith issued a statement that attempted to explain the traditional prohibition of women from the Roman Catholic priesthood. Entitled *Declaration of the Question of the Admission of Women to the Ministerial*

[1] Carroll Stuhlmueller, ed., *Women and Priesthood: Future Directions. A Call to Dialogue from the Faculty of the Catholic Theological Union at Chicago,* with a Foreword by Carol Francis Jegen (Collegeville, Minn.: Liturgical Press, 1978).

[2] Paul K. Jewett, *The Ordination of Women: An Essay on the Office of Christian Ministry* (Grand Rapids, Mich.: Wm. B. Eerdmans, 1980).

[3] For a list of books and articles published between 1960 and 1980 on the issue of women and the priesthood, see *Ordination of Women in Ecumenical Perspective,* Faith and Order Paper 105, ed. Constance Parvey (Geneva: World Council of Churches, 1980) 75-94. *Women and Priesthood,* 179-85, also contains a list of publications on the subject, prepared by Hyang Sook Chung Yoon, which includes five bibliographies.

Priesthood, it is known by its opening Latin words, *Inter Insigniores.*[4] Because of the manner of its pronouncement and publication, as well as its peculiar language and phrasing, the statement is taken by the authors of *Women and Priesthood* as nothing more than an opinion, albeit a weighty one, of the Vatican's official doctrinal congregation approved by Pope Paul VI. As an opinion, it is open to debate; as the opinion of the Roman Church's "Holy Office," it is to be vigorously debated because, the Chicago Catholics contend, it is fundamentally erroneous. Their collection of critical essays represents as thorough a rejection of it as can be made from within the Roman Catholic Church.

The book by Paul K. Jewett, the best work on the subject by a Protestant, favors the ordination of women to all churchly ministries, including the Roman Catholic priesthood.[5] "Destined to be a classic,"[6] It is enthusiastically prefaced by a Roman Catholic nun who calls for the ordination of women to the priesthood of her Church. It also contains a detailed critique of *Inter Insigniores.* To be fully appreciated, this book by the Professor of Systematic Theology at Fuller Theological Seminary in California should be studied together with his earlier work on human sexuality, *Man as Male and Female.*[7] Both books are of particular interest to the Orthodox because their "evangelical" author presents his case primarily on the basis of his understanding of the biblical doctrine of God.

The Context of the Debate

When reading books and articles on the subject of the ordination of women, including the works referred to here, one quickly becomes convinced that virtually everyone enters

[4]This document is published in full in *Women and Priesthood,* 212-25.

[5]The author shows little interest in Orthodoxy. His arguments, however, are certainly intended to apply to Orthodox as well as to Roman Catholics and Protestants (see 77-8).

[6]According to Nancy Hardesty of Emory University, as quoted on the front cover of *The Ordination of Women.*

[7]*Man as Male and Female* (Grand Rapids, Mich.: Wm. B. Eerdmans, 1975).

this debate with a conviction about the truth of the matter and what ought to be done about it. The "material" of the debate—scriptural texts, patristic treatises, conciliar decrees, canonical laws, historical events—are interpreted in the light of this conviction, and the arguments for or against the ordination of women are presented accordingly, using the sources to defend that position. This does not mean that those involved in the debate are dishonest and prejudiced, but rather that they are, quite understandably and naturally, formed by a tradition that provides and shapes their general vision of things. This general vision results from a combination of theological, moral, liturgical, ecclesial, social and cultural experiences that come together to produce a basic "feeling" and "intuition" about the way things are and ought to be, in the light of which one interprets the words and actions of others, especially those of the past, including those ascribed to God in the Bible.

Fr. Georges Florovsky has dealt with this point in his writings.[8] So has Vladimir Lossky, particularly in his reflections on the meaning of tradition, to which we will refer below. What we want to affirm now is our conviction that no one really thinks, decides and acts on the issue of women and the priesthood (or, for that matter, on any other issue) in a vacuum. Everyone does so from within a living tradition, in a lived situation and vital context. No one comes to the "data" of the debate in a thoroughly detached and disinterested manner. Data by itself, as Fr. Florovsky has said, is "mute."[9] It responds to questioning and cross-examining. And the questioning and examining are always in a situation, from a perspective and toward a point. It cannot be otherwise. This is the only human way.

The "lived situation" of the Orthodox in the debate about women and the priesthood is radically different from that of Roman Catholics and Protestants, evangelical or liberal, high church or low. An Orthodox becomes quickly convinced of

---

[8]See "The Predicament of the Christian Historian" in *Christianity and Culture: Volume Two in the Collected Works of Georges Florovsky* (Belmont, Mass.: Nordland, 1974) 31-65.
[9]Ibid., 36.

this when he or she participates in the debate. It can be claimed, as Aleksei Khomyakov claimed more than a century ago, that the Roman Catholic and Protestant "lived situations" are much more comparable and compatible with each other than either is with the Orthodox.[10] This may not seem so on the surface of things because of the external similarities between Roman Catholics and Orthodox, especially in regard to the priesthood. But the theological struggles between Catholics and Protestants, with their common Western European and American histories, their common ways of approaching theological and sacramental issues, their common manner of treating the Bible and their common definitions, categories and general ways of thinking—even with all of the disagreements *within* these ways—does make for greater understanding and agreement between them, even when their understanding is that there is real disagreement. This does not exist between members of these churches and the Orthodox.

Khomyakov made a further point in the middle of the last century, and this point is also, in my view, of inestimable significance today, particularly in regard to the issue of women and priesthood. He predicted that the time would inevitably come when Roman Catholics would no longer accept the authority of the Vatican over their religious and intellectual lives, and that when this happened, such Roman Catholics would show themselves to be thoroughly "Protestant" in their spirit and approach to God, Christ, the Church and the Christian life in general. He said that this would occur because when the authoritarian superstructure of Rome is shaken, most members will not have a sufficiently strong sense of doctrinal and spiritual "collegiality" to prevent them from splintering into individualistic and subjectivistic teachings and pieties; nor will their sacramental and liturgical experience be strong enough to unite them freely in one common churchly mind. I believe that Khomyakov's prediction has come true in our time, and I offer as a prime example

[10]See Aleksei Stepanovich Khomyakov, "On the Western Confessions of Faith," in *Ultimate Questions: An Anthology of Modern Russian Religious Thought,* ed. Alexander Schmemann (New York: Holt, Rinehart & Winston, 1965) 31-69.

of this, among the countless examples that might be presented in the area of professional theology, the work of the Catholic Theological Union at Chicago on women and the priesthood.

What characterizes the "Protestant" theological spirit and method, which we now see adopted by many Roman Catholics, is more than anything else its acceptance of the world and its history as providing the vital context for theological thought and analysis. The Church is reduced to a historical "religious institution," the tradition of the Church is reduced to historical actions and decrees, and both the Church and tradition (including the Bible) become "objects" of theological examination and reflection. Such a spirit and approach is the exact opposite of the traditional Christian practice, which the Orthodox, who have not themselves been westernized, still claim to retain.

For the Orthodox, as for the "prescholastic" Christian tradition in general, the Church is experienced in history as the fulness of life, of grace and of truth, of the kingdom of God, which provides the living context for theological thought and analysis. As such, the Church is the "subject" of theological thought and activity, with the secular world and human history being among the many "objects" of her examination, evaluation and judgment. In this perspective, or rather in the *experience* that gives rise to this perspective, the Church is essentially known and lived as a sacramental community with an identity and continuity in space and time guaranteed to her by the action of God's Holy Spirit. It is the life of the Holy Spirit in the Church which is her Holy Tradition. This tradition is not reducible to church history, still less to a collection of historical documents and acts. And the issue of what tradition is and how it operates, particularly in relation to the Bible, lies at the very heart of the debate about women and the priesthood.

The Bible and Tradition

In *Women and Priesthood,* Carolyn Osiek writes that the "way in which Tradition becomes normative and yet develops and unfolds new ways of understanding is precisely what is at issue in this book."[11] This is certainly true. Theologians in the Orthodox Church have often defended the fact that many things must change in the Church, and must be constantly changing, in order for the Church herself to remain the same. And it is easy to demonstrate that great changes have occurred in the forms and expressions of Christian faith and life in Orthodox Church history over the centuries. One need only compare the celebration of the eucharist in the time of the apostles with the divine liturgies of the Byzantine and Russian empires to see this. The issue at hand, therefore, is not one of change as such. It is rather of identifying how and in which ways the Church changes in order to remain truly herself, truly the same. It is the issue of determining which changes are imperative, in order that Christians may indeed remain "loyal to the faith given in Jesus Christ," and which changes are in fact betrayals of that faith, which corrupt and damage Christ's Church.

The methods by which Christians show themselves "loyal to the faith given to them in Jesus Christ," while changing and adapting their structures and practices in order to remain loyal, depends, strictly speaking, on what their faith is and how it lives within the ecclesial community to which they belong. Put in these terms, the debate about women and the priesthood is, in a real sense, a debate about the Christian faith itself.

The "liberals" in all the churches have the least trouble with the issue of fidelity and change. Put much too simply, though adequately I believe for our present purposes, Christian "liberals" affirm Lowell's stirring message that "new occasions teach new duties, time makes ancient good uncouth; they must onward still and upward, who would keep abreast of truth." Thus, they are ready, on the basis of their "scientific studies" in the light of "historical developments," to identify what they find new and beneficial in society with the inspiration and action of the Holy Spirit, while rejecting what they consider old and harmful as being opposed to the will of

[11]*Women and Priesthood*, 68.

God, even when such may be the teachings of the Scriptures, recorded even as coming from Jesus himself.

"Evangelical" Christians, on the other hand, are traditionally obliged to demonstrate that the changes they advocate in church teaching and practice are in strict conformity with the words and spirit of the Bible. In this tradition, the changes required in church life are necessarily considered as "reformations," that is, "corrections" in doctrine and practice. These changes are required of Christians in order for them to remain loyal to the faith given in Jesus Christ when the Scriptures have been wrongly interpreted and when true biblical teachings have been perverted and betrayed.

In what can be called the "neo-evangelical" movement, in which I would locate Professor Jewett, the tendency has developed to replace the Scriptures as such with the "Word of God," or the "gospel," or the "original teachings of Jesus," and to identify corruptions in the canonical writings themselves of this pure message. Thus, one follows the Paul of the "original gospel," who in the debate about women and the ministry is known primarily, if not exclusively, as the author of Galatians 3:28, while one rejects the Paul who slides back to the pre-evangelical standards of "rabbinic Judaism" in other of his writings—which in the debate about women amounts to virtually all of the other sayings attributed to him. This distinction in the canonical New Testament writings between pure, evangelical Christianity and impure hangovers from old covenant Judaism—or impure developments in newly developing "catholic" Christianity—is, as I understand it, something new for "evangelical" Christians. Its cause seems surely to be the inability, and/or the unwillingness, of its proponents to defend a purely "biblical" line in the classical, conservative Protestant manner, with no other available method of dealing with the texts and the issues within the Protestant tradition except that of the "liberal" alternative.

There is also a sense, in my view, in which contemporary Roman Catholics who have been freed from the authoritarian guidance of the Vatican find themselves in virtually the same theological position as Protestant "neo-evangelicals." Roman

Catholics generally claim that their doctrines and practices are thoroughly biblical. Their traditional position, however, has been that the Bible is interpreted ultimately by the magisterium of the Church, which has been instituted by God for this purpose. The magisterium, which in the final analysis is the papacy, determines which changes in the Church are according to the Scriptures and in the spirit of Christ, and which are not. The changes which are considered to be in harmony with the biblical testimony must also be in harmony with traditional "official" teachings and practices of the Roman Church, which have already been affirmed as enjoying this privilege. If, in our instance, the ordination of women were to be accepted by the Church's teaching authority, it would have to be demonstrated as being something that the Bible supports, or at least does not deny, but which has not been undertaken in the past for purely historical and cultural reasons. It can in no way be considered as being a "correction" or "reformation" of something that was officially taught and practiced by the Church, which by definition is always necessarily "loyal to the faith given in Jesus Christ."

In recent times, a doctrine of the "development of dogma" has been elaborated in Roman Catholic theology which proves very helpful for this issue. The teaching allows the Church to claim that a doctrine and/or practice not known in the Christian past may emerge at some point in history when it is needed in order for the Church to remain faithful to herself and to the teachings of the Lord. The emergence of the new dogma in the new historical situation is considered to be the work of the Holy Spirit, and discerning the signs of the times by the inspiration of the Spirit is a prerequisite for the new dogma's recognition, formulation and acceptance. Thus, for example, the early Church did not teach or practice the infallibility of the bishop of Rome as defined in the nineteenth century by Vatican Council I and now practiced in the Roman Catholic Church. But God guided the Church by his Holy Spirit into the present teaching in order for her to be enabled to protect and defend the teachings of Christ and his people in the new situations and circumstances. If there is such "dogmatic development," the argument runs, even to the point of such a major change in ecclesiastical structure and expression, as is the modern papacy in comparison with the ecclesiastical organization of the early Church, then it is quite possible that the ordination of women to the priestly and episcopal offices is a contemporary "dogmatic development" required by the Lord and inspired by his Spirit. What needs to be demonstrated—and this is the whole point of the "dialogue" called for by the Catholic Theological Union at Chicago—is that indeed the development of the priestly and episcopal ordination of women is now required. What the Vatican still holds, as the declaration of the Holy Office in October 1976 demonstrates, is that such a move is not considered a legitimate development, but rather an act of betrayal. What virtually all sides in the debate within the Roman Catholic Church generally agree upon, however, is that the final word, in either case, belongs to the magisterium, as *Inter Insigniores* insists: "In the final analysis it is the Church, through the voice of her Magisterium, that in these various domains, decides what can change and what must remain immutable."[12]

The Orthodox Church does not have a teaching of "dogmatic development." Orthodox believe that expressions of Christian faith and life can change and indeed must change as the Church moves through history. But the Orthodox interpret these changes as being merely formal and not in any sense substantial. They would never agree that there can be anything in the Church of Christ today that was not essentially present at any moment of the Church's life and history.

The Orthodox also do not have a magisterium that speaks finally on any matter of faith and practice. People sometimes think that the ecumenical council holds the place of the magisterium in the Orthodox Church. This is not true, or at best is only partially correct. A council in the Orthodox Church becomes "ecumenical" and its decisions and decrees become "binding" on all members of the Church when it has been universally accepted by all churches that recognize each other as Orthodox—and when, thereby, it is incorporated into the Church's official liturgical celebration. There have

---

[12]*Inter Insigniores* 23, in *Women and Priesthood,* 218.

been cases in Orthodox Church history when councils of
hundreds of bishops have been rejected by the Church. And
other cases exist where small, provincial councils have been
universally received. The only thing approaching a "magisterium" in the Orthodox Church, therefore, is the universal
agreement of all of her members, which is normally arrived
at only after decades, if not centuries, of controversy—and,
at least in the past, seldom without dissension, division,
persecution and even blood. This conviction, that the guardian
of the truth of Christ in and for the Church is the entire body
of the faithful, was explicitly stated in the famous encyclical
letter of the Eastern Orthodox patriarchs in 1848 in reply to
the epistle of Pius IX to the Eastern Churches. In this letter
the Orthodox bishops state clearly that "neither Patriarchs
nor Councils could . . . have introduced novelties amongst
us, because the protector of religion is the very body of the
Church, even the people themselves, who desire their religious
worship to be ever unchanged and of the same kind as that
of their fathers."[13]

For the Orthodox there is neither "development of
dogma" nor a "magisterium" that exists over, or even within,
the body of the faithful to guarantee the correct interpretation of the Scriptures. There is simply the Church herself in
her living sacramental and spiritual tradition, mystically
actualized in her liturgy, realized in her saints, witnessed by
her martyrs, defended by her confessors, articulated by her
fathers and councils and always protected and preserved by
the entire body of her members. In this sense the Church's
tradition is not a collection of texts, documents or decrees,
nor is it the sum total of her historical decisions and actions.
It is rather the living truth of God, or the truth of God living
within the entire body of the faithful. Or, perhaps most accurately, it is as Vladimir Lossky has put it, the Church in her
"unique mode of receiving [the truth]."[14] As such, the tradi-

[13]*Encyclical Epistle of the One, Holy, Catholic and Apostolic Church to
the Faithful Everywhere, Being a Reply to the Epistle of Pius IX to the
Easterns. Dated January 6, 1848* (South Canaan, Penn.: Orthodox Book Center,
1958) 25.
[14]Vladimir Lossky, *In the Image and Likeness of God*, eds. John H. Erick-
son and Thomas E. Bird (Crestwood, N.Y.: SVS Press, 1974) 151.

tion provides the living context within which all theologizing is done in the Church, and all decisions are made. It is neither magic nor mechanical; it does not operate according to some set of fixed patterns and rules. It is a free and, in the classical sense, a "charismatic" phenomenon. Because it is of God and his Christ and his Spirit, it cannot be otherwise. Lossky explains it this way:

> . . . to Tradition in its pure notion there belongs nothing formal. It does not impose on human consciousness formal guarantees of the truths of faith, but gives access to the discovery of their inner evidence. It is not the content of Revelation, but the light that reveals it; it is not the word, but the living breath which makes the words heard at the same time as [being] the silence from which it came; it is not the Truth, but a communication of the Spirit of Truth, outside which the Truth cannot be received. . . . The pure notion of Tradition can then be defined by saying that it is the life of the Holy Spirit in the Church, communicating to each member of the Body of Christ the faculty of hearing, of receiving, of knowing the Truth in the Light which belongs to it . . .[15]

On the issue of the ordination of women, therefore, the Orthodox will decide if the Church's present practice of ordaining only certain of her male members to the presbyterate and episcopate is in accordance with the will of God only if and when this practice is challenged from within the Church by any of her members, and is defended in any act by any of her bishops. Only then will it be seen if indeed the present practice is merely a historical and cultural accident or a dogmatic truth from God. Until now no voice has arisen anywhere within the Orthodox Church claiming that women ought to be ordained as priests and bishops. And the reason for this, to my mind, is not that the issue has yet to catch up with the Orthodox. It is rather that the body of the faithful recognizes that the life and faith of the Church, inspired

[15]Ibid., 151-2.

and guided by the Spirit of God in her Holy Tradition, precludes such a development, whether or not the theological reasons for this have as yet been articulated in a clear and convincing manner.

The Vision of God

The most important arguments concerning women and the priesthood, which should prove ultimately decisive in the debate, are drawn from teachings about God. Loosely speaking, most proponents of the ministerial ordination of women promote some version of "process theology" in which God and the world are changing in such a way as to call for the "full inclusion" of women in all leadership positions in church and society at the present moment of history. However, neither the Chicago Catholics nor Professor Jewett are in a line of "process theology"; instead, both develop arguments supporting the ordination of women on the foundation of their doctrine of God. In his book on the ministry, taken together with his work on human sexuality, *Man as Male and Female,* Professor Jewett makes about as perfect an argument for the ordination of women drawn basically from the Bible as can be made. If one agrees with the vision of God presented in these books, both the Catholic and the "neo-evangelical," then one is compelled, I would think, to defend the ordination of women to every church ministry, including the priesthood and episcopate. The argument, presented so well and so convincingly is, as I understand it, basically the following.

The one, true and living God is an asexual spirit (or supra-sexual supra-spirit) who is known in three personal forms, traditionally called Father, Son and Holy Spirit. The three forms of divinity have nothing to do with God's essential being and nature, yet they do nevertheless manifest the critically important fact that there is real diversity and variety in God's being and action. Human beings, male and female, are made in the image and likeness of God. Within human nature the two forms of human being, masculine and feminine, have nothing to do with one's basic humanity, but do confirm the fact that there is a real diversity and variety within human nature that images the divine Trinity. Since Christian ministry exists for human beings to do the work of God, and even, in a sense, to "image" God's presence in church and society, the ministry must be performed by persons of both sexes in order for it to be truly complete and effective.

The maleness of Jesus, in this argument, has nothing to do with the ordained Christian ministry, both as "working" and "imaging." Jesus the Messiah, as God's incarnate Word on earth and the glorified Lord of God's kingdom in heaven, is fundamentally and essentially *human,* not male. Thus, the ministers of the Church who express Christ's essential human-ity and accomplish his essentially human activity must be both men and women for God-in-Christ to be most adequately imaged and for his work to be most adequately accomplished. This is particularly so in the present time, especially in the West, where the full realization of who, what and how God really is is finally being properly comprehended and actualized in the structures of church and society due to the maturation of humankind brought about by the inspiration of God acting in history.

The problem with this kind of argumentation, from the Orthodox Christian perspective as I understand it, is that the vision of God, and of the ministry derived from it, is funda-mentally incorrect. The argument is a powerful one. It is carefully and cleverly drawn and appears most compelling and convincing. But it is basically wrong. It is wrong because its vision of God is essentially a *modalistic* one, to use tradi-tional categories. And, quite logically, it produces a *modalistic* vision of humanity as well.

Strictly speaking, according to Orthodox theology, again as I personally understand and teach it, God is not to be con-ceived as "one God in three persons," or as "three persons in one divine substance," if this is taken to mean that the one God is expressed in three personal forms so that it is one and the same God who is understood as being the Father, Son and Holy Spirit. Strictly—and I would say, biblically, liturgic-ally and creedally—speaking, the one, true and living God is

not Father, Son and Holy Spirit. He is the one God and
Father who has within himself eternally and, one might dare
say, as an "element" of his very being and nature, his only-
begotten Son, also called his divine Word and Image, who—
being another person or hypostasis than who God is—is
incarnate as the man Jesus, the Christ of Israel and the
Savior of the world. This one God and Father also has within
him his one Holy Spirit, who proceeds from him alone and
rests eternally in his Son and Word, anointing him in his
incarnate manhood to be the messianic King, and through
him, personally indwelling and deifying those who belong
to him and his Father. The vision is one of three distinct
divine persons or hypostases who are confessed, as in the
Nicene Creed, to be the "one God, the Father almighty" and
the "one Lord Jesus Christ, the Son of God, the only-begotten
. . . of one essence with the Father," and "the Holy Spirit,
the Lord, the Giver of Life, who proceeds from the Father."
It is this God whom the Orthodox Church addresses in her
eucharistic liturgy in this manner:

> For Thou art God . . . Thou and Thine only-begotten
> Son and Thy Holy Spirit. . . .

> For all these things we give thanks to Thee, and to
> Thine only-begotten Son, and to Thy Holy Spirit . . .

> Holy art Thou and All-holy, Thou and Thine only-
> begotten Son and Thy Holy Spirit.[16]

The divine "Thou" of Orthodox worship is the one God and
Father. His Son is also a "Thou," as is his Holy Spirit. And
the three are divine. This is the biblical teaching, summarized
in the creed and celebrated in the liturgy. The Father and
the Son and the Holy Spirit are three equally and identically
divine persons or hypostases. They are "of one essence" or
"nature." There is no metaphysical superiority of any of the
persons to the others, and no ontological subordination. Yet
the one God and Father is the source of his Son and Spirit.

---

[16]Anaphora of the Liturgy of St. John Chrysostom.

And the Son and Spirit are not only "from the Father" ontologically (by way of "generation" and "procession"), but are personally obedient to him in their divine being and activity. They do his will, they carry out his work, they complete his actions, they reveal his person, they communicate his nature, they bring him to creation and take creatures to him. This does not mean that they are any less "divine" (or any less "God," to speak in this way) than the Father. And this certainly does not diminish or degrade them in any manner at all. On the contrary. It is to their everlasting glory, honor and worship that they are, from all eternity, God's very own Son, Image and Word and his own Holy Spirit.

In his actions in and toward the world of his creation, the one God and Father reveals himself primarily and essentially in a "masculine" way. This is the biblical and liturgical mode of expression, which cannot be altered or abandoned without changing and ultimately destroying the revelation itself. The eternal Father of the only-begotten Son becomes, through his Son and in his Holy Spirit, the Father of all human beings made in his divine image and likeness. The Father is said to be "maternal" in his actions, more tender and loving than the most perfect human mother. Yet he is *Father,* and not *Mother.* And his only-begotten *Son* (not *Daughter*) is the bridegroom of the Church, his Spirit-filled bride—the head of his churchly body with whom he becomes "one flesh" in the Spirit. The Son and Word of God relates to creation (made by, for and in himself) in a masculine, and not a feminine, manner. He is incarnate in human masculine form to embrace and redeem the entire creation, filling all things with all the fulness of divine life to be his beloved body and bride. This is the biblical message, whose language and symbolism have permanent theological, spiritual, mystical and liturgical significance and value.

The error in the theology presented in the literature favoring the ordination of women to the priesthood, including the essays by the Catholic scholars from Chicago and especially the marvelous books by Professor Jewett, is that the trihypostatic Godhead is not seen and appreciated for what it really is, and the traditional biblical symbols of divine revelation, enshrined in the classical creeds and celebrated in the classical liturgies, come completely undone. They are emptied of their significance and power. They are rendered void of meaning and application in the human community, including the sacramental community of the Church, which is traditionally seen and experienced by the Orthodox as the "recreation of creation," the kingdom of God on earth.

The divine nature is certainly sexless. And certainly all human beings, male and female, are made in the image and according to the likeness of God. Every human person is logical and spiritual—that is, each human being has, and in a sense *is*, both word (logos) and spirit. And every human person who is part of the original creation redeemed and sanctified in the Church is made to image the one God and to do his work on earth, which is, in Christ and the Holy Spirit, a priestly, prophetic and kingly ministry, whatever one's sex or vocation. But in the Church, the specific ministry of being the presbyterial/episcopal head of the sacramental community, which is by grace the "recreated creation," is the specific ministry of imaging the person and effecting the ministry of the Son and Word of God incarnate in human form, in his specifically "masculine" being and activity. The sacramental priest is not the image of God or divinity in general. He is certainly not the image of the Trinity or of the Holy Spirit. He is the image of Jesus Christ, who makes known the Father in the Spirit within the life of God's Church. And this "image" can only be actualized and effected by certain male members of the Church, who are called and equipped for this ministry.

The Issue of "Natural Resemblance"

It may appear that the position presented here is the same as that found in the argument concerning the need for "natural resemblance" in the sacraments as articulated in the Vatican declaration, *Inter Insigniores*. Or it may seem to be but another version of the argument often made by the defenders of the masculine priesthood of the "iconic" nature of the sacramental minister, who is the living "icon" of the masculine Jesus. The Vatican document puts the argument this way:

> The whole sacramental economy is in fact based upon natural signs, on symbols imprinted upon the human psychology: "Sacramental signs," says Saint Thomas, "represent what they signify by natural resemblance." The same natural resemblance is required for persons as for things: when Christ's role in the Eucharist is to be expressed sacramentally, there would not be this "natural resemblance" which must exist between Christ and his minister if the role of Christ were not taken by a man: in such a case it would be difficult to see in the minister the image of Christ. For Christ himself was and remains a man.[17]

This argument, if it refers simply to male biology, or as Thomas More Newbold, C.P., says in *Women and Priesthood*, to "sexual anatomy,"[18] is wholly unconvincing. The point to be made is not that the priest has to "look like Jesus." It is rather that there must be something in the very nature of the person to be ordained that allows him to be the sacramental presence of the Lord, the mystical embodiment of the Church's husband and head. Water bears no "natural resemblance" to the cosmos as a whole, nor to a womb or a tomb, which the baptismal waters represent and symbolize. Yet water is the perfect matter for the baptismal mystery because of what it is in the everyday life of human beings. And oil has no "natural resemblance" to the person of the Holy Spirit, who comes upon the newly baptized in chrismation. Yet sanctified chrism is surely the perfect material sign for accomplishing the mystery of pentecostal sealing. And bread and wine bear no "natural resemblance" to flesh and blood, except perhaps in the most superficial and artificial way, yet they are the proper foods for the sacramental presence of the Lord's body and blood in the eucharist, used by Jesus himself at the supper

[17]*Inter Insigniores* 5:27; see *Women and Priesthood*, 219-20.
[18]P. 133.

as recorded in the synoptic gospels and the first letter of St.
Paul to the Corinthians.

The priest does not bear a "natural resemblance" to Jesus
in his biological and anatomical maleness. But to be the
proper sacramental presence of Jesus the priest must be a
once-married or celibate man, a sound Christian, whole in
body and soul, without scandal and of good reputation both
within and without the community of the faithful; a masculine person capable of heading the body with the compassionate wisdom and sacrificial love of a husband and father. Such
a position, obviously, is based on the conviction that there is
such a reality as fatherhood and husbandship, and that to be
father and husband in and to an ecclesial community is a
masculine spiritual activity that a woman, by nature and
vocation, cannot and should not be expected to fulfil. The
point is not about "natural resemblance." It is rather about
natural competence.

The priest is certainly a member of the Church. But he is
not ordained and consecrated to "represent" the Church—just
as he is not appointed to "represent" God. He is rather ordained and appointed to make the person and action of
Jesus Christ sacramentally present in and for the Church.
For this reason the priest has traditionally been called *alter
Christus* in a very specific way. He is said to act *in persona
Christi,* and even to "hold the place of God," as God himself
heads his final covenant community with his people in the
person of his glorified Son whom he has made Messiah and
Lord through his high-priestly sacrifice on the cross. In this
way, too, the priest has also traditionally been called *Father,*
since through Jesus he actualizes the personal Fatherhood of
God in the community, as do all fathers in all families, since
it is from God alone that "every family [πατριά, literally
"fatherhood"] in heaven and on earth is named" (Eph 3:15).

Not every Christian man is called to be a priest, though
theoretically and ideally every one might be. No woman is
ever called to this vocation—her very womanhood precludes
it, since she cannot possibly be a husband and father. The
key to the vocation of women as women, in my view, is
theologically and mystically discovered in the person of the

Holy Spirit, whose divinity is identical to that of the Father and the Son, but whose unique form of divine existence is different from that of the two other divine hypostases. The Holy Spirit is the divine person who proceeds from the Father and rests in the Son, and through the Son is given to the world, inspiring and sanctifying the whole of creation to become Christ's body and bride. The "icon" of the Spirit is the Church, and the personal expression and "icon" of the Spirit in the Church is the Virgin Mary. There is a point, in my view, to the theological and spiritual association of the Holy Spirit with the feminine in the order of creation, just as there is reason to associate the masculine with Jesus Christ, the Son and Word.

But whatever one's opinions about sexuality in the created world being metaphysically and mystically grounded in the uncreated divine hypostases of Son and Spirit, it is my conviction that no argument can be made for a feminine priesthood in relation to the Holy Spirit, since the priesthood is that of Christ and not the Spirit—just as there can be no argument for a merely "human" priesthood on the basis of the asexual nature of divinity as such.

The Significance of Secular Development

The final argument made by the Chicago Catholics and Professor Jewett in their formidable writings is drawn from the significance of contemporary secular developments regarding women and the ministry. Their point is simply that women in our time have come to positions of leadership in all areas of the secular community through the undeniable action and will of God. In the past, even in biblical times, according to Carroll Stuhlmueller, the noted Dominican scriptural scholar and editor of *Women and Priesthood,* the people of God took the key for their structural organization from the societies in which they lived and through which the Lord constituted them as his people, challenging them in their developing and ever-changing fidelity to his words and actions in history.[19] This means that today the churches are called to structure themselves on the pattern of secular, primarily western and westernized, societies where women function as leaders in all areas of life. Women must be allowed to function as bishops and priests, as well as pastors, ministers, teachers, administrators and executives in all ecclesiastical bodies. If they are not allowed to assume such positions and duties, the argument runs, the churches will not only lose their credibility in the modern world as a liberating force in support of justice and equality for all, especially for the oppressed and exploited, but they will clearly be disobeying their Master and Lord, who is calling them to this action. And, in addition, they will fail to realize their truly *eschatological* nature, in which all distinctions between male and female are finally overcome, and secular society will, in this sense, be in greater conformity with God's will than are his own churches.

In the view of Jewett, and of many others who favor women's ordination, the Christian Church has done much, despite its sins, to improve the lot of women in the world. But it has "drawn back, being conformed to this world at one crucial point," he writes. "We refer, of course, to the church's withholding from the women the office of ministry with the authority and privilege which such an office implies."[20] The idea here is that the failure of the Church to ordain women to the presbyterial/episcopal office has been a "conforming to this world," which should never have happened in the beginning, and that presently, ironically, the world has gone beyond the Church, or at least most of the churches, in opening positions of authority and privilege to women as well as men.

My thoughts on this point are exactly the opposite of Professor Jewett's and of those who agree with him. It seems to me that the Church was actually *resisting* conformity to this world in her practice of ordaining only certain of her baptized men to the presbyterial/episcopal office. The societies in which the Church lived, in both the old and new covenants, certainly knew female leadership. Israel itself had

---

[19]See *Women and Priesthood*, 35.
[20]Jewett, *Ordination of Women*, 100.

women judges and queens, as did the empires and nations in which Christianity developed and reigned as the "official religion." But even in times when women ruled empires and were consecrated by the Church for this purpose and were canonized saints by the same Church for their successful service, there were no women priests or bishops in the Church. The question is, why not? And the answer, it seems to me, can only be because the Church has *theological* and *spiritual* reasons for her actions, which are intended to preserve, and not to deny, her eschatological character.

The Church exists in the world to proclaim and preserve a vision of God and the world, and a vision of men and women, within the fallen conditions of this age whose form is passing away (1 Co 7:31). Essential to this vision is the conviction that human nature images the nature of God within the conditions of creation in two forms: masculine and feminine. It insists that men and women are essentially identical in their humanity, but are not interchangeable in their completion and perfection of it. And it holds that there must be in the Church, since it does not always exist in the world, the clear expression of the distinction of the sexes in their mutual fulfilment through communion in love, which has nothing to do with privilege, power, prestige and authority. It is therefore the sign of the Church's ultimate *resistance* to this world—her calling not to be "conformed to this world" but to be "transformed by the renewal of . . . mind" in order to demonstrate "what is the will of God, what is good and acceptable and perfect" (Rm 12:2)—that the Church has not ordained women to her priestly and episcopal ranks. In this act the Church is drawing a line between herself, as the presence of God's kingdom in this world, and the world itself, as fallen in corruption, caught "in the power of the evil one" (1 Jn 5:19). It is truly ironic, in my view, that this age, which most Christians of Roman Catholic, evangelical Protestant and Eastern Orthodox traditions consider to be one of history's most unhappy, insane and disordered, would be raised up by theologians as providing the pattern for the Church's own being and life.

The Issue of Our Time

The question of women and the priesthood is but one important instance of what I see to be the most critical issue of our time: the issue of the meaning and purpose of the fact that human nature exists in two consubstantial forms: male and female. This is a new issue for Christians; it has not been treated fully or properly in the past. But it cannot be avoided today. How we respond to it, I believe, clearly demonstrates what we believe about everything: God and man, Christ and the Church, life and death. It is, in a manner of speaking, our particular issue for controversy: our gnosticism or Arianism, our Origenism or iconoclasm. It is the issue of our time, the issue that inevitably comes to every age and generation "in order that those who are genuine . . . may be recognized" (1 Co 11:19). It is our controversy for judgment.

The Orthodox Church has hardly begun to formulate her response to the issue, but she must take it up and complete it. It is, I believe, not a task of discovering *what* the truth is— it is rather the task of articulating and explaining it in proper theological language and concepts. It is the perennial theological task of finding the "words adequate to God." Just as the Church *knew* the Father, Son and Holy Spirit to be equally divine and praiseworthy, but required centuries to forge out the proper and convincing formulation of the dogma of the suprasubstantial Trinity, so, it seems to me, the Church *knows* what she believes and practices concerning men and women in the life of the Church, including the priesthood, but it appears certain that it will take years of theological labor for her to arrive at a fitting dogmatic statement to explain and defend it.

The works of the Roman Catholic and Protestant theologians are of inestimable importance in assisting us Orthodox Christians in our task. We must be truly grateful for all who have had the concern and the courage to become involved in the debate.